'TIS THE AUTUMN SEASON

FALL QUILTS AND DECORATING PROJECTS

Jeanne Large and Shelley Wicks

Martingale®
Create with Confidence

'Tis the Autumn Season:
Fall Quilts and Decorating Projects
© 2013 by Jeanne Large and Shelley Wicks

Martingale®
19021 120th Ave. NE, Ste. 102
Bothell, WA 98011-9511 USA
ShopMartingale.com

Printed in China
18 17 16 15 14 13   8 7 6 5 4 3 2

Library of Congress Cataloging-in-Publication Data is available upon request.

ISBN: 978-1-60468-247-2

MISSION STATEMENT

Dedicated to providing quality products and service to inspire creativity.

CREDITS

President & CEO: Tom Wierzbicki
Editor in Chief: Mary V. Green
Design Director: Paula Schlosser
Managing Editor: Karen Costello Soltys
Acquisitions Editor: Karen M. Burns
Technical Editor: Laurie Baker
Copy Editor: Tiffany Mottet
Production Manager: Regina Girard
Illustrator: Ann Marra
Cover & Text Designer: Adrienne Smitke
Photographer: Brent Kane

CONTENTS

Bonus Project Online! *Download "Harvest Spice Trio" at ShopMartingale.com/extras—a free pattern for coordinating tea towels, coasters, and apron.*

INTRODUCTION

Why not surround yourself with what you love? This is our philosophy regarding using quilts in our homes. Quilts can be so much more than bed coverings. They can be a wonderful decorating tool, no matter if your home is modern, contemporary, or country. Quilts can fit into any decor.

We enjoy the process of designing and making a quilt. Because we enjoy it, we do it a lot. Consequently, we've accumulated a lot of quilts. These quilts overflowed from the bedrooms—where we started using them—into other rooms, and for purposes other than just keeping warm. We realize decorating with quilts is not a new idea, but it never hurts to be reminded that it's a great idea.

Here on the prairies where we live, we celebrate every change of season. And while it's sad when summer comes to an end, we look forward to the beautiful, rich, autumn colors we appreciate outdoors. It's the perfect time to pull out the quilts with fall colors and continue Mother Nature's color scheme indoors. Of course, winter was made for snuggling up with a quilt and our favorite warm beverage while we enjoy a book or watch the snow fall. And when Old Man Winter finally slips back into hiding and new growth appears from the ground, out come the table toppers and wall hangings with flowers and buds that remind us that a season of newness is near.

Just a small project like a pillow or a table runner can add a seasonal touch to any room. Or try some quilts outdoors when enjoying cool evenings. Wherever and however you use your quilts, the important things are using them, enjoying them, and being motivated to make more.

We hope the ideas and projects we share in 'Tis the Autumn Season will inspire you to be creative in both your quiltmaking and home decorating. We've tucked in a few of our favorite family recipes to warm your soul as well. Give them a try on a crisp, fall day!

~ Jeanne and Shelley

DECORATING YOUR HOME WITH QUILTS

Quilting is more than a hobby. We see quilting as an expression of our creativity and sense of style. Whatever flavors your quilts are—country, contemporary, modern, or traditional—they'll no doubt reflect your decorating style. Whatever colors you love to sew with are likely the colors you use to decorate your home. Consequently, your quilts could appear in any room in your home and belong there.

Show them off! Why hide all your quilts in bedrooms? Every quilt is a work of art and a labor of love. The days of making a quilt out of necessity have been replaced by days of making quilts for the sheer pleasure of sewing and creating. So when we enjoy the creating of a quilt we want to enjoy using it as well.

Sometimes a customer in our shop will say, "I'd love to make that quilt, but what would I do with it?" Well, you can sit on it, lay on it, roll up in it, take a nap with it, fold it on top of a shelf, roll it up into a basket, hang it from a railing, lay it on a table, or give it away! The options are endless.

We enjoy quilts everywhere in our homes and think you should too. Here are some ideas, from our homes to yours.

The front porch is a great place to start. What better way to welcome people to your home than with a few quilts. If your porch is open you may want to wait to put things out until you're expecting guests. If your porch is enclosed, you can truly showcase some of your favorite quilts. Fold a quilt over the back of a chair or lay a quilt on a love seat (and yes, *sit on it!*). Add a couple of pillows, a runner, or a framed quilt project. Summer evenings can be cool so it's nice to have a couple of quilts in a nearby basket so we can enjoy those longer days.

Whether you have a front porch or not, you can make the entryway to your home warm and welcoming by using some of your quilts. Perhaps you have a railing to drape a quilt over, a table to use a runner on, or a basket to roll a quilt into. There's a difference between cluttered and cozy, so you may need to experiment with some of your projects to achieve the feeling you want to express in your decorating.

Photos below: (Left) Group quilts together to make a statement. (Center) A single quilt draped over a railing brings a casual feeling to any room. (Right) Keep a quilt or two within easy reach for cool mornings and evenings relaxing on the porch.

Most of us have our favorite items in our favorite rooms. It only makes sense to surround ourselves with things we love in the space in which we spend the most time. So if you spend much time in the kitchen, add some of your favorite quilts, or make something that will work in your space. The kitchen is a perfect room to display a runner or table topper. Do you have a rocking chair or a favorite space to sit down with a cup of coffee? Draping a quilt over the back of a chair will give the room a relaxing feeling without taking up any wall space.

When we say "off the beds and onto the table" we mean it literally. A dining room tends to be a room with large pieces of furniture, often very dark furniture, and lots of straight lines. You can soften this look with a quilted wall hanging, a table runner, or a quilt on the table. Try it! You'll be amazed at the comments you receive. A quilt on the table is truly a "show off." It doesn't matter if it's one of your finest pieces or a scrappy-leftovers project, your room will have a more comfortable feeling. You may want to remove the quilt before dining, or use place mats at each place setting.

For many of us, our favorite room in our house isn't the kitchen but the family room or living room. This is a space that truly cries out for the comfort of quilts. If space is limited, you could hang quilts on a ladder. This allows you to feature a couple of quilts without taking up much space.

The quilts you want people to use should be handy; on the back of the couch, folded on the back of a favorite chair, or stacked in a basket. A quilt that's been washed a couple of times will look more inviting than one that is crisp and new. It's so easy to change the seasonal look of a room just by changing the quilts. Sometimes the quilt backing can be just the color you need, so go ahead and fold the quilt with the backing showing.

Your sewing room may be your favorite room. If your sewing room is full of projects waiting to be finished or waiting to be started, you may find some inspiration and motivation if you cleared out a space for some finished quilts. Stacking some folded quilts on top of a cupboard or shelf will remind you that you *can* and *do* finish things. This is a great place to store out-of-season quilts rather than folded in a closet where no one ever sees them.

Decorating Your Home with Quilts

If you like to entertain outdoors, the patio or deck is a great spot to show your work. A hard wooden bench looks far more appealing with a quilt folded on it, and a huge Adirondack chair is much more comfortable with a pillow in it.

Use a quilt on a table where you're serving dry snack foods or over the back of a wooden bench. Mother Nature provides the perfect decorating scheme to display your quilts, so anything goes.

One of the greatest pleasures we receive from quilting is to give one away. It doesn't matter if you're giving it to a dear friend, a new grandchild, or a charity—it's a gift from the heart. It's wonderful to have just a few quilts on hand for those occasions. A quilt given as a gift needs no wrapping paper. Just roll it up and tie it with ribbons!

If you have quilts stashed away, now is the time to audition them in various rooms in your house. If it just doesn't suit your home, maybe it will suit the home of a friend. Every quilt is made with love . . . pass it on.

Photos below: (Facing page left) Containers are a great way to store and display several quilts at once. (Facing page center) Set the tone of the room with several quilts that use the same theme. (Facing page right) A quilt draws immediate attention to a table.

(Below left) Keep quilts that you want to use easily accessible. (Below center) Bring inspiration into your sewing room with a stack of your favorite quilts. (Below right) Every quilt fits into Mother Nature's decorating scheme.

FABRIC SELECTION AND PREPARATION

Fabric is what quiltmaking is all about, so selecting the right fabrics is the key to a great-looking quilt.

FABRIC SELECTION

Choosing the fabrics for a new project is intimidating for a lot of people. Indeed, it's the most important step toward an attractive quilt. Of course, the most important component is good-quality fabrics. No matter if your color preference is earth tones, brights, or pastels, using a good-quality fabric will ensure those colors are still beautiful after multiple washings and much use.

If you find the process of choosing fabric a scary endeavor, then enlist the help of your local quilt shop. It's always a good idea to have a color theme in mind, but be open to ideas and suggestions. Don't be afraid to voice your likes and dislikes. In the end, it's your quilt, not the salespersons!

We like to lay out bolts of fabric on a table so we can see and get an overall feel for the finished quilt. If you'll be adding fabrics from your stash, be sure to have them with you while shopping. It's a good idea to go into a new project thinking "maybe" a piece of fabric from home will work. Depending on how long you've had that fabric, it may be difficult to match. Colors change every year according to trends, so a fabric that's five years old could have different coloring than what's available now. Bring it along when you go shopping, but don't be too surprised if it doesn't fit into your new project.

If possible, it's helpful to view all your fabric selections for the project together. Be critical. Does it have the overall look you want? Does the accent fabric truly read as an accent? Is there some variety in the designs of the fabrics (some large prints, some small prints)? Don't be afraid to mix dots, prints, stripes, and plaids. Do you like the overall look? Be sure. If there's a fabric in your project you don't really care for, it's far easier to replace it now before you start than to regret using it when the quilt is finished. If you're selecting your fabrics at home, it may be beneficial to leave them for a while, and then come back for a second look. If something is out of place

or just doesn't belong, it will jump out at you when you see it with fresh eyes.

Scrappy quilts are a contradiction to everything we hold near and dear regarding fabric selection. When it comes to making a scrap quilt, it seems you can break every rule about color choice and placement. However, it's still a good idea to be somewhat selective in your scrap choices. Being careful in the choosing will result in a project that is cohesive and pleasing to the eye overall.

PREWASHING—DO I HAVE TO?

We all have a lot of laundry to do already so why add to the load? Pardon the pun!

There are lots of reasons we don't prewash our fabrics. First of all, we love the feel of fabric fresh from the bolt. The finish applied to fabric that gives it that feel also makes it easier to cut and sew. We also don't have to worry so much about shrinkage and bleeding, which used to be the main reasons for prewashing. Good, quilt shop-quality fabrics have a very minimal shrinkage rate and the colors are unlikely to bleed from one piece to another. Nowadays, we also have a huge variety of precut fabric available to us, and there are some you definitely wouldn't prewash: 5" squares, 10" squares, and 2½" strips. They're much easier to work with in their fresh-from-the-manufacturer precut sizes. So, in the interest of efficiency and enjoyment of quilting, we don't prewash our fabrics.

It's important to remember that prewashing is a personal choice. There's no rule regarding washing yardage. The saying "better safe than sorry" may apply to a piece of fabric you have that you feel unsure about. But remember, you'll lose some fabric to fraying so be sure you purchase a large enough piece to accommodate laundering if you decide to prewash.

We don't prewash our quilt batting or backing either. The look we love is that overall scrunched-up softness you get when you wash a newly finished quilt. It's a look that says, "Cuddle up and keep warm."

BASIC QUILTMAKING TECHNIQUES

Knowing the basics will take you a long way to creating a beautiful finished project. This is the section to refer to if you need to brush up on your skills, learn a few new ones, or indulge in some special techniques to broaden your quilting horizon.

ROTARY CUTTING

All the projects in this book require the basic tools of quiltmaking: a rotary cutter, mat, and ruler. There are many brands and sizes to choose from, so you must decide for yourself what will suit your needs, taking into account the availability of products, your budget, and the amount of space you have. Some quilters purchase every ruler available, while others are minimalist in their needs. The ruler we like to work with is 6" x 24". This will accommodate most cutting, and makes it easy to cut your fabric as it's folded from the bolt. For smaller needs, such as crosscutting strips, the 6" x 12" ruler is handy. As for a rotary cutter, it's really a matter of preference. The 45 mm rotary cutter is the standard and by far the most practical if you plan to own only one. When it comes to mats, bigger is better. A mat measuring 24" x 36" will allow you to cut several strips without moving the fabric or folding it more than once. If you find yourself in doubt over a product, visit your local quilt shop; they are sure to have knowledgeable staff to answer your questions.

1. The most important step in accurate cutting is to start with a straight edge. You may hear this referred to as "squaring up your fabric." Start by folding the fabric in half, aligning the selvages. Lay the fabric on the cutting mat with the selvages closest to you and straight along a horizontal line on your mat. The left edge of the fabric should be lying on the left end of your mat with the excess fabric to your right. (Some people like to cut the opposite way—try both and see which feels better to you.)

2. Align your acrylic ruler (preferably 6" x 24") along a vertical line on your mat so that all the raw edges of the fabric are covered by the edge of the ruler. With your hand firmly on the ruler and your pinkie finger against the far outside edge to prevent slipping, use the rotary cutter to cut along the right edge of the ruler. Discard this strip of fabric. Your fabric is now straightened and ready to be cut. Measure and cut your pieces from this edge.

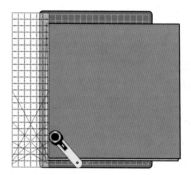

3. Measuring from the straightened edge, cut strips the width given in the pattern instructions. We like to use the lines on our mat as well as the lines on our ruler for added accuracy. For example, if you need a 2½"-wide strip, place the 2½" vertical line of the ruler on the straightened edge of the fabric, making sure the ruler is lined up along vertical lines on the mat.

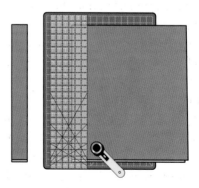

4. To crosscut the strip into squares or rectangles, open up the folded strip and trim away the selvage. Lay the strip along a horizontal line on the mat. Line up the ruler against the lines on your mat like you did with the larger fabric piece. Measure the required length and cut your sections.

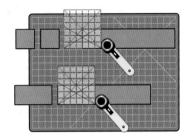

MACHINE PIECING

An accurate ¼" seam allowance is a key factor in quilting. Accurate piecing will ensure that your blocks fit together and you'll be happy with the finished product. Even a very small amount of error will multiply until your rows won't fit together like they should. Many sewing machines come with a ¼" presser foot. If your machine doesn't have one or if you want to check the accuracy of your presser foot, it's a simple process.

Lay an acrylic ruler under your presser foot. Be sure the ruler is straight. Line up the edge of the ruler with the edge of the presser foot. Gently lower the needle. It should land on the ¼" mark on the ruler. If not, adjust the ruler until the point of the needle is aligned with the ¼" mark. Carefully lay a piece of masking tape along the edge of the ruler to mark the ¼" mark, being careful not to cover the feed dogs with the tape. Align the edge of the fabrics with this taped mark when feeding fabric through the machine.

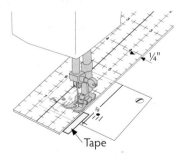

STRIP PIECING

We like to use strip-piecing techniques to speed up the piecing process. This is especially useful when making checkerboard blocks or anything with numerous repetitive pieces.

To make a strip set, sew strips together in the required fabric combinations. Press the seam allowances toward the darker fabric or as indicated in the pattern. Then, straighten one end of the strip set and cut the remainder of the strip into the required-size segments.

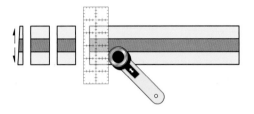

CHAIN PIECING

Chain piecing is a quick and efficient method of piecing multiple units that are the same. Feed the units through your machine continuously, without stopping or cutting the thread between units. When you have the number of units required for your project, remove the chain and snip the threads between the units. Press according to the pattern instructions.

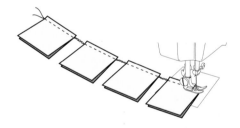

PRESSING SEAM ALLOWANCES

Careful pressing is just as important as accurate piecing. Good pressing techniques will help your blocks lie flat and fit together well.

There are various opinions on whether or not to use steam. We prefer an iron that steams well; however, when using the steam setting on your iron, be extra careful when moving the blocks so you don't stretch them. If your block is a bit misshapen, a good spray starch and some steam can work wonders.

1. Lay the pieced unit on the ironing board with the fabric you want to press toward positioned on top. Unless your pattern tells you different, you should press toward the darker fabric. Briefly bring the iron down onto the closed seam. This sets the seam.

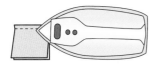

2. Lift the iron and fold the top piece of the unit back to expose the seam line. Press the seam flat from the front. The seam allowances will now lie flat under the fabric that was originally positioned on top.

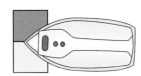

When sewing rows of blocks together, it's helpful to press the seam allowances in opposite directions from row to row. This will help your seams lie flatter and lock into each other.

We adore appliqué—easy, chunky appliqué of course. (Nothing too time consuming or delicate for us!) Here we'll share two of our favorite and most-used methods. Fusible-web appliqué is an easy trace-cut-and-fuse method. Edges are finished with hand or machine stitching. Fusible-interfacing appliqué gives your shapes a turned-under edge that is then blind-stitched in place.

We'll also explain how we make stems and vines, as well as how we incorporate rickrack into our appliqué repertoire.

FUSIBLE-WEB APPLIQUÉ

There are many varieties of fusible web on the market, so you may have to try several before you find the one that will work best for your project's needs. We highly recommend using a lightweight, paper-backed product. Anything too heavy tends to gum up your sewing-machine needle, is too hard to sew through, and will add a stiff feeling to your quilts. Be sure to read the instructions that come with the product for guidelines on heat settings and fusing times.

When using fusible web, you need to be sure the shapes are reversed from the patterns shown on the completed quilt. The patterns in this book have already been reversed for you.

1. Using a pencil, trace the appliqué shapes onto the paper side of the fusible product, leaving at least 1" between shapes.
2. Cut the appliqué shapes out of the fusible web, approximately ¼" outside of the pencil lines. If a shape is large, cut out the fusible web from the center of the piece, leaving ¼" to ½" inside the pencil line. This helps keep your appliqué pieces soft to the touch when the stitching is finished.

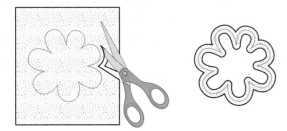

3. Follow the manufacturer's instructions to fuse each shape, paper side up, to the wrong side of the desired fabric. Press—don't iron. You don't want your shapes moving around.

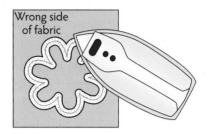

Wrong side of fabric

4. Allow the fabrics to cool. Carefully cut out each appliqué piece directly on the drawn line. Remove the paper backing from each piece.

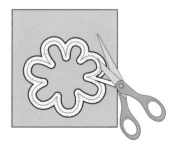

5. Working on your ironing board, arrange the shapes onto the background fabric, referring to the pattern for proper placement. Be sure all shapes are tucked under or overlapped where they should be. Press the appliqués in place.
6. Sew the raw edges of all the appliqué shapes to the background fabric either by hand or machine. The stitch we most commonly use is a blanket stitch. Using a thread color that matches the appliqué pieces will make your stitching almost invisible; using a dark charcoal or black thread gives a more primitive look.

FUSIBLE-INTERFACING APPLIQUÉ

This is a great method to use for large shapes with gentle curves. We don't recommend it for small, delicate shapes.

Before you start a project using fusible interfacing, you may want to test various brands—one manufacturer's version of a lightweight product may be another one's version of a mediumweight product. Test a few and find the one that works best for you. The fusible interfacing remains in the appliqué, so it's important to use one that is easy to work with, but won't make your appliqué feel overly stiff. We recommend a light- to mediumweight woven or nonwoven interfacing, depending on your preference.

1. Using a pencil, trace the appliqué shapes onto the non-fusible side of the fusible interfacing, reversing the shapes if necessary and leaving at least 2" between shapes.

2. Cut the appliqué shapes out of the fusible interfacing, approximately 1" outside of the pencil line.

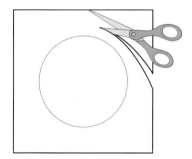

3. Lay a fusible-interfacing shape with the fusible side against the right side of the chosen fabric; pin in place. Sew directly on the drawn line around the entire shape.

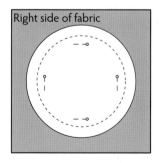

Right side of fabric

4. Trim around the shape leaving approximately a ⅛" seam allowance all around. Carefully make a slit in the center of the fusible interfacing, long enough to be able to turn the shape right side out.

5. Once the shape is turned, gently run your finger, or a blunt object, around the inside of the shape along the seam line to help ease the edges out. The fusible side of the product is now facing out, and the raw edges are on the inside. Arrange your shape on the background fabric, referring to the pattern for proper placement. Gently press the appliqué in place with a hot iron.

6. If your sewing machine has a blind hem stitch in its functions, you can program that stitch so the point of the V just nips into the appliqué. Using an invisible thread will give the look of hand appliqué. Another option is to blanket-stitch by hand or machine.

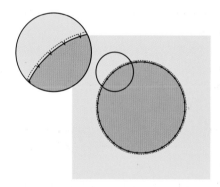

Blind hem stitch

WOOL APPLIQUÉ

We use a fusible product to appliqué with felted wool, but the freezer-paper method is a good alternative. If the project will be laundered, then fusing the shapes down and stitching the edges will provide more durability. For something like a pillow or wall hanging that may not need to be washed, using the freezer-paper method may be a good choice.

FUSIBLE-WEB METHOD

Follow the instructions on page 12 for making appliqués from cotton fabric, but keep the following pointers in mind:

- Be sure to read the product instructions carefully. If your iron is too hot, you'll scorch the wool.

- If you find it difficult to fuse the wool appliqué shape to the cotton background fabric, try pinning it in place, flipping the project over, and pressing well from the back. The heat will easily penetrate the cotton and melt the glue, fusing down the wool shape.

- If you're layering wool appliqué shapes, we've found it works best to fuse one layer at a time.

FREEZER-PAPER METHOD

If you plan to stitch wool appliqué shapes by hand, you may prefer to use the freezer-paper method.

1. Trace the appliqué shapes onto the non-shiny side of the freezer paper. Cut around the shapes, leaving about ½" of paper outside of your pencil lines.

2. Lay the shiny side of the freezer paper onto the wool and gently press down with a dry iron on a medium setting. The wax on the freezer paper will melt enough to stick the paper to the wool.

3. Cut out the shape directly on your drawn line. Peel the freezer paper off and your wool shape is ready to be hand stitched to your project.

WORKING WITH WOOL

We love hand-dyed felted wool. It comes in an array of delicious mottled colors and because the fabric has already been felted, it's ready to use when you purchase it. Felting simply means that the wool has been washed in hot water and agitated, and then dried in a hot dryer. This process shrinks the wool and locks the fibers together, so the fabric won't ravel or continue to shrink with subsequent washings. Felted wool doesn't usually have a right side or a wrong side; both sides generally look the same.

SPECIAL TECHNIQUES

Taking the time to add a little extra zing to your project is often what makes it shine. Adding something special doesn't have to be difficult. Often it's the simplest additions that will add the most to a project. This section is where you'll find the fun techniques we've used in the projects throughout the book.

BIAS VINES

Cotton-fabric vines are easy to make and cutting them on the bias makes them easy to shape. We suggest starting with an 18" to 20" square of fabric.

1. Lay your fabric along the cutting mat and cut the square in half diagonally. If you have a 45° line on your cutting mat you can use it as a guideline. Using the diagonal line you've just cut as your guide, continue to cut diagonal strips of fabric. Usually a 1½"-wide strip will give you a bias vine that's wide enough to have good visual impact but narrow enough to manipulate easily.

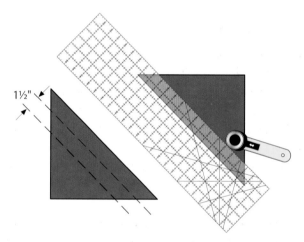

2. With right sides together, join the strips at right angles as shown to achieve the length required. Press the seam allowances open.

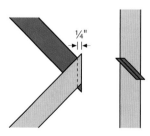

3. Lay the strip right side down on your ironing board. Press it in half lengthwise, wrong sides together.

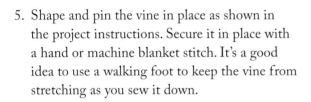

4. Fold the raw edges toward the folded edge of the long strip. Keep the raw edge slightly behind, not even with, the folded edge; press. The raw edges will be hidden beneath the vine, but you'll also have some flexibility in the width you choose to create your vine. Now you have a folded edge on both sides of your vine.

5. Shape and pin the vine in place as shown in the project instructions. Secure it in place with a hand or machine blanket stitch. It's a good idea to use a walking foot to keep the vine from stretching as you sew it down.

RICKRACK STEMS AND VINES

Rickrack makes wonderful vines or flower stems on a quilt. It comes in a variety of widths and a wide range of colors, so you have plenty of options. You also have several options when sewing it to your project. If you're using a narrow rickrack, just pin the rickrack in place and machine sew down the center of the strip. We recommend using a walking foot to avoid stretching the rickrack. If you're using a wide rickrack, sew the edges down on both sides so they won't roll up or distort in any way when your quilt is washed. Sew down the edges using a machine blanket stitch, a straight stitch, or our favorite method: drop your feed dogs and free-motion stitch the edges using matching thread.

Good finishing techniques are essential to the finished quilt. This section deals with the proper way to add borders and binding.

ADDING BORDERS

When your quilt top is complete and it's time to add the borders, we suggest you measure your quilt top to ensure that the size of borders the pattern tells you to cut is in fact what your quilt top is measuring up to be. Sometimes the difference in seam allowances can add a bit of discrepancy in the finished size of the quilt top.

Careful measuring will ensure that your quilt top will lie flat. Double-checking your measurements and adjusting the border lengths accordingly can help you avoid borders that are too tight or fall in waves. Be sure your quilt top is well pressed before measuring.

1. Lay the quilt top flat and measure through the vertical center and the vertical sides (not directly on the edge of your quilt, but in about 6"). If the measurements differ from each other, take the average of the three measurements and cut the two vertical borders to that length.

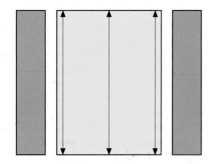

2. Fold the border strips in half crosswise to find the centers. Do the same with the quilt top. Pin the center of the borders to the center of the sides of the quilt top. Align the ends of the quilt top and the ends of the borders, pin in place. Add more pins between these pinpoints, easing any fullness or gently stretching as required.

3. Sew the borders to the sides of the quilt top. Press the seam allowances toward the borders.

4. Repeat this process for the top and bottom borders, measuring through the horizontal center and sides.

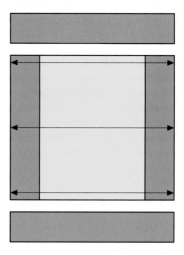

BINDING

All of our projects use double-fold binding made from 2½"-wide strips. The patterns in this book allow for enough binding to go around the perimeter of the quilt, plus extra for joining the strips and mitering the corners.

1. Cut the binding fabric across its width, unless otherwise specified, into the number of 2½"-wide strips required.

2. With right sides together, join the binding strips at right angles as shown to make one long strip. Trim the seam allowances to ¼" and press them open to reduce bulk.

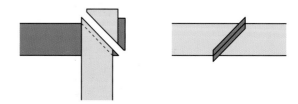

3. Cut one end at a 45° angle, turn that end under ¼", and press in place. Fold the strip in half lengthwise, wrong sides together, and press.

4. Place the end of the binding midway down one edge of the quilt. Align the binding raw edges with the edge of the quilt top and start sewing approximately 10" from the start of the binding strip. Sew through all the layers using a ¼" seam allowance, stopping ¼" from the first corner. Backstitch, clip the threads, and remove the quilt from the machine.

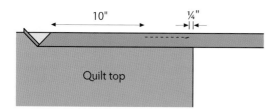

5. Turn the quilt so you're ready to sew the next side. Fold the binding straight up at a 90° angle away from the quilt, and then back down onto itself so the binding raw edge is even with the quilt edge again. Stitch from the fold, backstitching at the edge of the quilt. This fold will create a mitered corner when you turn the binding to the back of the quilt and blindstitch it in place. Continue sewing the binding to the edges of the quilt, repeating the mitering process at the remaining corners.

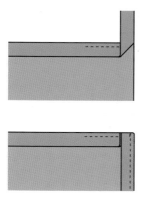

6. Stop sewing and backstitch when you're approximately 10" to 12" from where you started. Cut the remaining tail of binding at an angle 1" longer than needed. Tuck the tail into the starting diagonal edge. Finish sewing the binding.

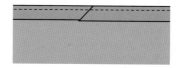

7. Bring the folded edge of the binding over to the back of the quilt, covering the raw edges of the quilt. Be sure the binding covers the sewing line. Use a thread that matches the binding and blindstitch in place, mitering the corners as you come to them.

REUNION

FINISHED QUILT: 72½" x 72½" ❀ **FINISHED BLOCK: 12" x 12"**

These vibrant thistle flowers pop as they dance among the luscious espresso-and-chocolate rows. Wool adds depth and texture to this rich quilt.

Designed and made by Jeanne Large and Shelley Wicks; machine quilted by Wendy Findlay

MATERIALS

Cotton yardage is based on 42"-wide fabrics; wool yardage is based on 54"-wide fabric.

¼ yard *each* of 12 assorted medium- to dark-brown fabrics for strip rows

2½ yards of light-brown fabric for Star blocks and appliqué background

1 fat quarter of charcoal felted wool for flower-center appliqués

½ yard of dark-red fabric for flower appliqués

½ yard of green fabric #1 for bias stems and leaf appliqués

½ yard of dark-brown fabric for Star blocks

⅓ yard of medium-dark brown fabric for Star blocks

¼ yard of medium-brown fabric for Star blocks

1 fat quarter (18" x 21") of green fabric #2 for flower-base appliqués

⅔ yard of dark-brown fabric for binding

4⅞ yards of fabric for backing

80" x 80" piece of batting

3 yards of 18"-wide lightweight paper-backed fusible web

Matching threads for appliqué

CUTTING

Cut all strips across the width of the fabric unless otherwise specified.

From the light-brown fabric, cut:

3 strips, 3½" x 42"; crosscut into 24 squares, 3½" x 3½"

1 strip, 4¼" x 42"; crosscut into 6 squares, 4¼" x 4¼". Cut each square into quarters diagonally to yield 24 triangles.

2 strips, 7¼" x 42"; crosscut into 6 squares, 7¼" x 7¼". Cut each square into quarters diagonally to yield 24 triangles.

4 strips, 12½" x 42"; crosscut into:
 3 rectangles, 12½" x 20½"
 3 rectangles, 12½" x 16½"
 3 squares, 12½" x 12½"

Continued on page 20

From the medium-brown fabric for Star blocks, cut:
1 strip, 4¼" x 42"; crosscut into 6 squares, 4¼" x 4¼".
Cut each square into quarters diagonally to yield
24 triangles.

From the medium-dark brown fabric, cut:
2 strips, 3⅞" x 42"; crosscut into 12 squares,
3⅞" x 3⅞". Cut each square in half diagonally to
yield 24 triangles.

From the dark-brown fabric for Star blocks, cut:
3 strips, 3⅞" x 42"; crosscut into 24 squares,
3⅞" x 3⅞". Cut each square in half diagonally to
yield 48 triangles.

From *each* of the 12 assorted medium- to dark-brown fabrics, cut:
3 strips, 2½" x 42" (36 total); cut the strips in half to
yield 2 strips, 2½" x 21" (72 total)

From the dark-brown fabric for binding, cut:
8 strips, 2½" x 42"

MAKING THE STAR BLOCKS

1. Sew each light-brown 4¼" triangle to a medium-brown 4¼" triangle along the long edges to make a half-square-triangle unit. Press the seam allowances toward the medium-brown triangle.

2. Arrange four half-square-triangle units from step 1 into two horizontal rows of two units each as shown. Sew the units in each row together. Press the seam allowances in alternate directions. Sew the rows together. Press the seam allowances in one direction. Repeat to make a total of six pinwheel units.

Make 6.

3. Sew a medium-dark brown 3⅞" triangle to opposite sides of each pinwheel unit. Press the seam allowances toward the triangles. Repeat on the remaining sides of the pinwheel units

to make the block center units. Square up each center unit to measure 6½" x 6½".

Make 6.

4. Sew dark-brown 3⅞" triangles to the short sides of a light-brown 7¼" triangle. Press the seam allowances toward the dark-brown triangles. Repeat to make a total of 24 star-point units.

Make 24.

5. Arrange one center unit, four star-point units, and four light-brown 3½" squares into three horizontal rows as shown. Sew the pieces in each row together. Press the seam allowances in the directions indicated. Sew the rows together. Press the seam allowances toward the top and bottom rows. Repeat to make a total of six blocks.

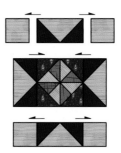 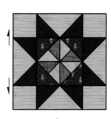

Make 6.

MAKING THE STRIP-PIECED ROWS

1. Randomly sew six assorted medium- to dark-brown 2½" x 21" strips together along the long edges to make a strip set. Press the seam allowances in one direction. Repeat to make a total of 12 strip sets. Crosscut the strip sets into 24 segments, 9½" wide.

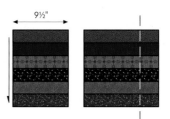

9½"

Make 12 strip sets.
Cut 24 segments.

2. Sew six segments together as shown to make a row that measures 9½" x 72½". Press the seam allowances in one direction. Repeat to make a total of four rows.

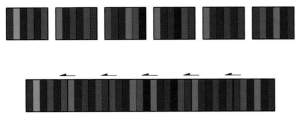

Make 4.

ASSEMBLING THE QUILT TOP

1. Arrange the strip-pieced rows, Star blocks, light-brown 12½" x 20½" rectangles, light-brown 12½" x 16½" rectangles, and light-brown 12½" x 12½" squares into rows as shown. Do not sew the pieces together yet.

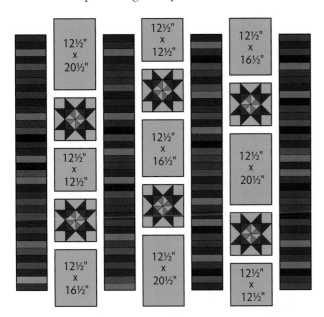

2. Refer to "Bias Vines" on page 14 for detailed instructions to prepare approximately 95" of bias stem from the green #1 fabric.
3. Refer to "Fusible-Web Appliqué" on page 12 and use the patterns on pages 22 and 23 to prepare the appliqués from the fabrics indicated.
4. Using the appliqué placement diagram above right and photo on page 18 as guides, pin the bias stems in place on the light-brown squares and rectangles. Arrange the appliqué shapes and

press in place, leaving off any leaves that overlap onto the strip rows or Star blocks. Use matching thread to blanket-stitch around each shape by hand or machine.

Appliqué placement

5. Sew the appliquéd rectangles, appliquéd squares, and the Star blocks in each vertical row together. Press the seam allowances toward the appliquéd rectangles and squares.
6. Pin and then sew the strip-pieced rows and appliquéd rows together. Press the seam allowances toward the appliquéd rows.
7. Refer to the photo to arrange the remaining leaf shapes on the quilt top and press them in place. Use matching thread to blanket-stitch around each shape by hand or machine.

FINISHING THE QUILT

Refer to "Finishing Basics" on page 16 for detailed instructions as needed.

1. Layer the backing, batting, and quilt top; baste.
2. Quilt as desired. Our quilt is machine quilted with an allover design.
3. Bind the quilt using the dark-brown 2½"-wide strips.

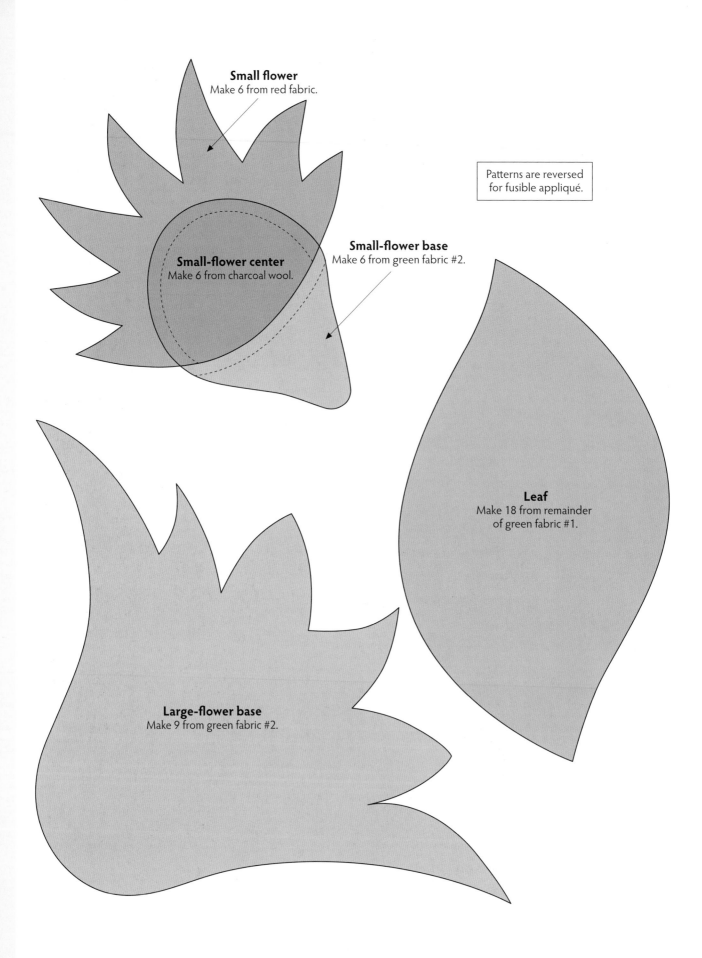

Small flower
Make 6 from red fabric.

Patterns are reversed
for fusible appliqué.

Small-flower base
Make 6 from green fabric #2.

Small-flower center
Make 6 from charcoal wool.

Leaf
Make 18 from remainder
of green fabric #1.

Large-flower base
Make 9 from green fabric #2.

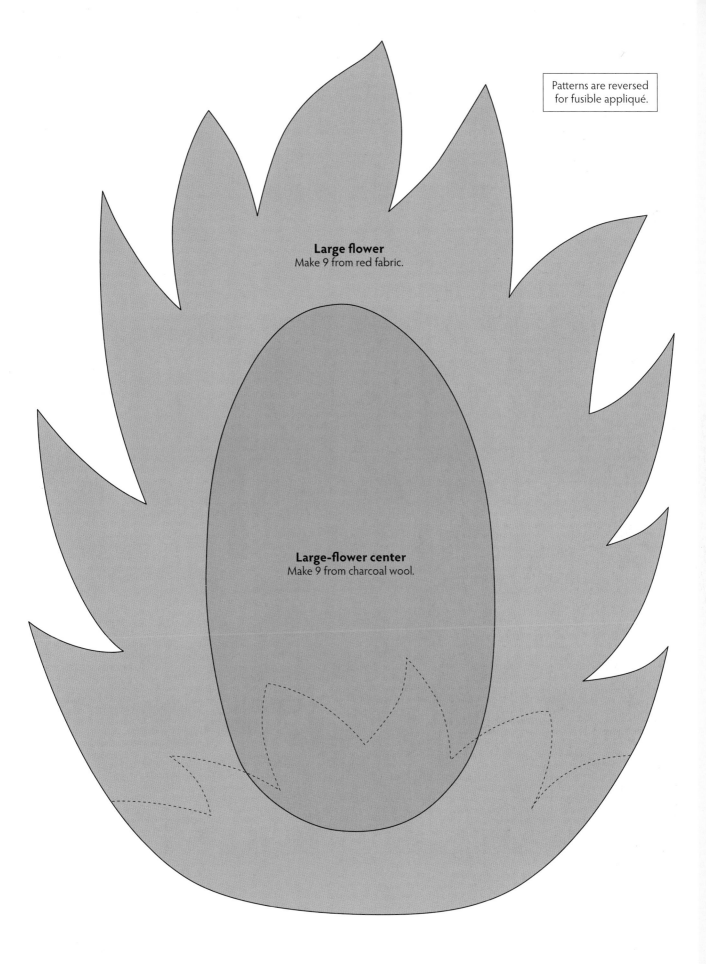

Large flower
Make 9 from red fabric.

Large-flower center
Make 9 from charcoal wool.

STELLA

Stella, Stella, Stella … with an abundance of flowers and offset quirkiness, this quilt's a looker whose rich colors look great in any season.

Designed and made by Jeanne Large and Shelley Wicks; machine quilted by Craig and Colleen Lawrence

MATERIALS

Yardage is based on 42"-wide fabrics.

15 fat quarters (18" x 21") of assorted gold, red, purple, and rust fabrics for Flying Geese blocks and flower appliqués

10 fat quarters of assorted beige fabrics for Flying Geese blocks

1⅝ yards of red print for outer border and binding

1⅛ yards of black tone-on-tone print for sashing and first and third borders

1 yard of beige tone-on-tone print for second border

1 fat quarter of gold print for flower-center appliqués

1 fat quarter of green print for leaf appliqués

4⅓ yards of fabric for backing

78" x 80" piece of batting

1½ yards of 18"-wide lightweight paper-backed fusible web

3⅓ yards of 1½"-wide green rickrack for vine

Matching threads for appliqué

CUTTING

Cut all strips across the width of the fabric unless otherwise specified.

From *each* of the 10 assorted beige fat quarters, cut:
3 strips, 4½" x 21" (30 total); crosscut into 12 squares, 4½" x 4½" (120 total)

From *each* of the 15 assorted gold, red, purple, and rust fat quarters, cut:
1 strip, 8½" x 21" (15 total); crosscut into 4 rectangles, 4½" x 8½" (60 total)

From the black tone-on-tone print, cut:
17 strips, 2" x 42"

From the beige tone-on-tone print, cut:
3 strips, 8½" x 42"
3 strips, 2" x 42"

From the red print, cut:
7 strips, 4½" x 42"
8 strips, 2½" x 42"

MAKING THE FLYING-GEESE ROWS

1. Use a pencil and a ruler to lightly draw a diagonal line from corner to corner on the wrong side of each beige 4½" square.

2. Layer one of the marked squares over one end of an assorted 4½" x 8½" rectangle as shown, right sides together. Sew from corner to corner directly on the drawn line. Fold the top corner back and align it with the corner of the rectangle beneath it; press. Trim away the excess layers of fabric beneath the top triangle, leaving a ¼" seam allowance. Repeat to make a total of 60 units. In the same manner, layer a marked beige square on the opposite end of each rectangle as shown, right sides together. Stitch, press, and trim as before to make 60 Flying Geese blocks.

 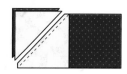

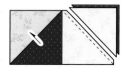 

Make 60.

3. Join 12 Flying Geese blocks along the long edges to make a row as shown. Press the seam allowances as shown. Repeat to make a total of five rows.

Make 5.

ASSEMBLING THE QUILT TOP

1. Sew the black 2" x 42" strips together end to end to make one long strip. From this strip, cut six strips, 2" x 48½"; two strips, 2" x 49½"; two strips, 2" x 61"; and two strips, 2" x 62".

2. Alternately sew the black 2" x 48½" sashing/first-border strips and flying-geese rows together side by side. Press the seam allowances toward the

black strips. Sew the black 2" x 49½" first-border strips to the top and bottom of the quilt top. Press the seam allowances toward the first border.

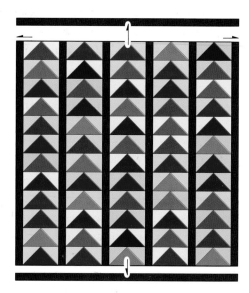

3. Sew the beige 8½" x 42" second-border strips together end to end to make one long strip. From this strip, cut one strip, 8½" x 51½"; one strip, 8½" x 49½"; and one square, 8½" x 8½".

4. Lay the beige 8½" x 51½" strip along the left side of the quilt top and the beige 8½" x 49½" strip along the top. Position the beige 8½" square in the corner between the two strips as shown. Using the illustration as a guide, arrange the rickrack along the length of the beige strips but not the corner square. Refer to "Rickrack Stems and Vines" on page 15 to sew the rickrack in place.

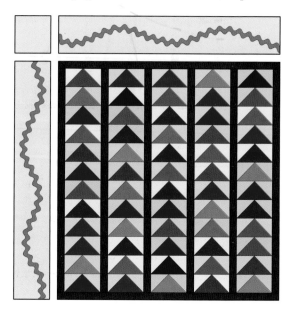

5. Refer to "Fusible-Web Appliqué" on page 12 and use the patterns on pages 28 and 29 to prepare the appliqués from the fabrics indicated.

6. Use the appliqué placement diagram below and the photo on page 24 as guides to arrange the appliqué shapes on the beige second-border strips and press them in place, being careful not to scorch the rickrack. Use matching thread to blanket-stitch around each shape by hand or machine.

7. Sew the left-side appliquéd second-border strip to the left side of the quilt top. Press the seam allowances toward the second border. Sew the 8½" square to the left end of the top appliquéd strip. Press the seam allowances toward the appliquéd strip. Sew the appliquéd second-border strip to the top of the quilt top. Press the seam allowances toward the second border. Appliqué the remaining large flower and leaves to the corner square, being sure to cover the ends of the rickrack with the flower.

Appliqué placement

8. Sew the beige 2" x 42" second-border strips together end to end to make one long strip. From this strip, cut one strip, 2" x 59½", and one strip, 2" x 59". Sew the 2" x 59½" strip to the right side of the quilt. Press the seam allowances toward the second border. Sew the 2" x 59" strip to the bottom of the quilt. Press the seam allowances toward the second border.

9. Sew the black 2" x 61" third-border strips to the sides of the quilt top. Press the seam allowances toward the third border. Sew the black 2" x 62" strips to the top and bottom of the quilt top. Press the seam allowances toward the third border.

10. Sew the red 4½" x 42" outer-border strips together end to end to make one long strip. From this strip, cut two strips, 4½" x 64", and two strips, 4½" x 70". Sew the 4½" x 64" strips to the sides of the quilt top. Press the seam allowances toward the outer border. Sew the 4½" x 70" strips to the top and bottom of the quilt top. Press the seam allowances toward the outer border.

Quilt assembly

FINISHING THE QUILT

Refer to "Finishing Basics" on page 16 for detailed instructions as needed.

1. Layer the backing, batting, and quilt top; baste.
2. Quilt as desired. Our quilt is machine quilted with an allover design.
3. Bind the quilt using the red 2½"-wide strips.

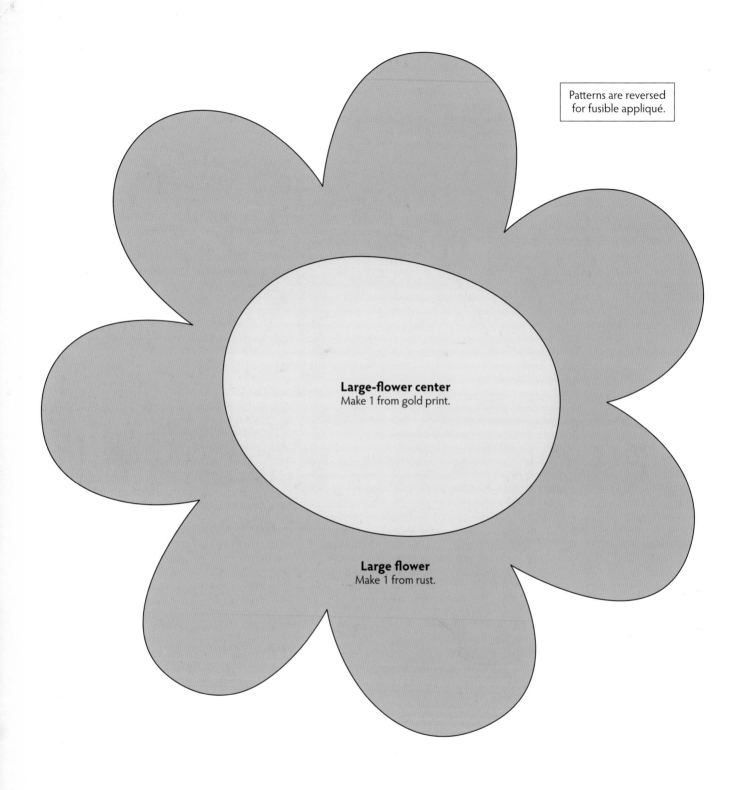

Patterns are reversed
for fusible appliqué.

Large-flower center
Make 1 from gold print.

Large flower
Make 1 from rust.

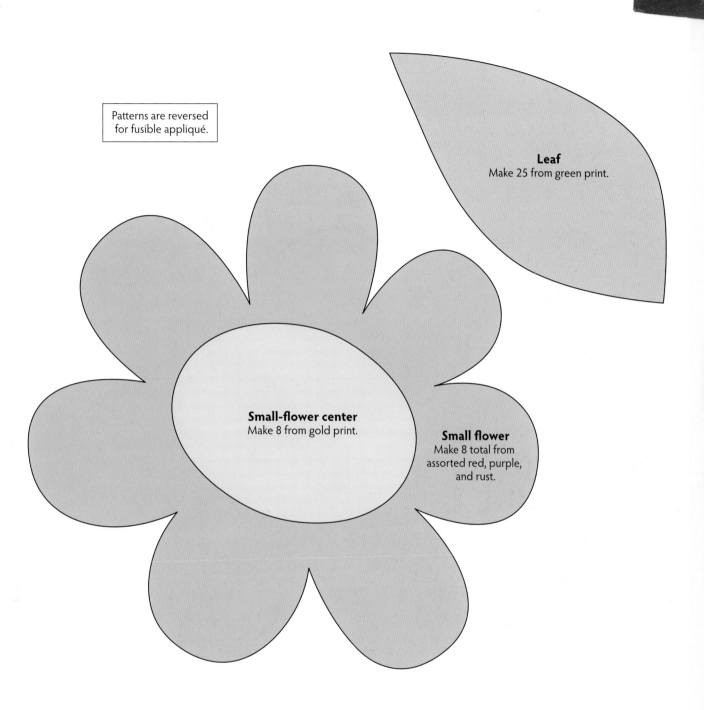

Patterns are reversed
for fusible appliqué.

Leaf
Make 25 from green print.

Small-flower center
Make 8 from gold print.

Small flower
Make 8 total from
assorted red, purple,
and rust.

STELLA'S BASKETS

FINISHED QUILT: 46½" x 46½" ❀ FINISHED BLOCK: 16" x 16"

Rickrack stems and perky red posies will light up any room on a chilly day, whether you display this quilt on a table or the wall.

Designed and made by Jeanne Large and Shelley Wicks; machine quilted by Wendy Findlay

MATERIALS

Yardage is based on 42"-wide fabrics.

1⅛ yards of cream fabric for appliqué block backgrounds

1⅛ yards of brown print for sashing, inner border, and outer border

⅝ yard of green fabric for middle border and binding

¼ yard of red fabric for stars

12" x 16" rectangle of brown fabric for basket appliqués

9" x 10" rectangle of dark-brown fabric for basket rim appliqués

10½" x 11" rectangle *each* of 3 assorted red fabrics for flower appliqués

10" x 11" rectangle of green fabric for leaf appliqués

7" x 15" rectangle of gold fabric for flower-center appliqués

3 yards of fabric for backing

55" x 55" piece of batting

1⅔ yards of ⅝"-wide green rickrack for stems

1¼ yards of 18"-wide lightweight paper-backed fusible web

Matching threads for appliqué

CUTTING

Cut all strips across the width of the fabric unless otherwise specified.

From the cream fabric, cut:

2 strips, 16½" x 42"; crosscut into 4 squares, 16½" x 16½"

From the red fabric, cut:

2 strips, 1½" x 42"; crosscut into 40 squares, 1½" x 1½"

1 strip, 2½" x 42"; crosscut into 5 squares, 2½" x 2½"

From the brown print for sashing and borders, cut:

6 strips, 2½" x 42"; crosscut into:
    4 strips, 2½" x 16½"
    4 strips, 2½" x 34½"
    8 rectangles, 1½" x 2½"
5 strips, 3½" x 42"

From the green fabric for middle border and binding, cut:

4 strips, 1½" x 42"; crosscut into:
    4 strips, 1½" x 34½"
    4 squares, 1½" x 1½"
5 strips, 2½" x 42"

APPLIQUÉING THE BLOCKS

1. Refer to "Fusible-Web Appliqué" on page 12 and use the patterns on pages 34 and 35 to prepare the appliqués from the fabrics indicated.

2. Using the appliqué placement diagram below and the photo on page 30 as a guide, pin the rickrack stems in place on a cream 16½" square. Arrange the prepared appliqué shapes on the square and press in place, being careful not to scorch the rickrack. Use matching thread to sew a straight line down the center of each rickrack stem. Use matching thread to blanket-stitch around each shape by hand or machine. Repeat to make a total of four blocks.

Appliqué placement

ASSEMBLING THE TABLE TOPPER

1. Use a pencil and a ruler to lightly draw a diagonal line from corner to corner on the wrong side of each red 1½" square.

2. Layer one of the marked squares over one end of a brown 2½" x 16½" strip as shown, right sides together. Sew from corner to corner directly on the drawn line. Fold the top corner back and align it with the corner of the brown strip beneath it; press. Trim away the excess layers of fabric beneath the top triangle, leaving a ¼" seam allowance. Repeat to make a total of four units. In the same manner, layer a marked red square on the adjacent corner of each strip as shown, and stitch, press, and trim as before to

make four star-point units. Set aside the remaining marked 1½" squares.

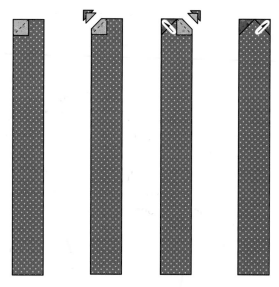

Make 4.

3. Arrange the four star-point units from step 2, one red 2½" square, and the appliquéd blocks into three horizontal rows as shown. Sew the pieces in each row together. Press the seam allowances toward the appliquéd blocks and red square. Sew the rows together. Press the seam allowances toward the block rows.

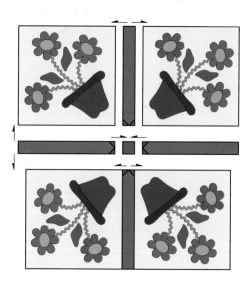

4. Repeat step 2 using the brown 2½" x 34½" strips and the marked red 1½" squares you set aside in step 2, making star points on both ends of the

strips. Make four inner-border strips. Set aside the remaining marked 1½" squares.

Make 4.

5. Sew an inner-border strip to the sides of the table topper. Press the seam allowances toward the table topper center. Join a red 2½" square to each end of the remaining two inner-border strips. Press the seam allowances toward the squares. Add these strips to the top and bottom of the table-topper. Press the seam allowances toward the table-topper center.

6. Layer one of the remaining marked red 1½" squares over one end of a brown 1½" x 2½" rectangle as shown, right sides together. Sew, press, and trim in the same manner as you did for the star-point units. Repeat to make a total of eight middle-border star-point units.

Make 8.

7. Sew a middle-border star-point unit to each end of a green 1½" x 34½" middle-border strip. Press the seam allowances toward the green strip. Repeat to make a total of four strips.

Make 4.

8. Refer to the table-topper assembly diagram to sew a middle-border strip to each side of the table-topper top. Press the seam allowances toward the inner border. Sew a green 1½" square to each end of the two remaining middle-border strips. Press the seam allowances toward the squares. Sew these strips to the top and bottom of the table-topper top. Press the seam allowances toward the inner border.

9. Sew the brown 3½" x 42" outer-border strips together end to end to make one long trip. From this strip, cut two strips, 3½" x 40½", and two strips, 3½" x 46½". Sew the 3½" x 40½" strips to the sides of the table-topper top. Press the seam allowances toward the outer border. Sew the 3½" x 46½" strips to the top and bottom of the table-topper top. Press the seam allowances toward the outer border.

Quilt assembly

FINISHING THE QUILT

Refer to "Finishing Basics" on page 16 for detailed instructions as needed.

1. Layer the backing, batting, and quilt top; baste.
2. Quilt as desired. Our quilt is custom quilted.
3. Bind the quilt using the green 2½"-wide strips.

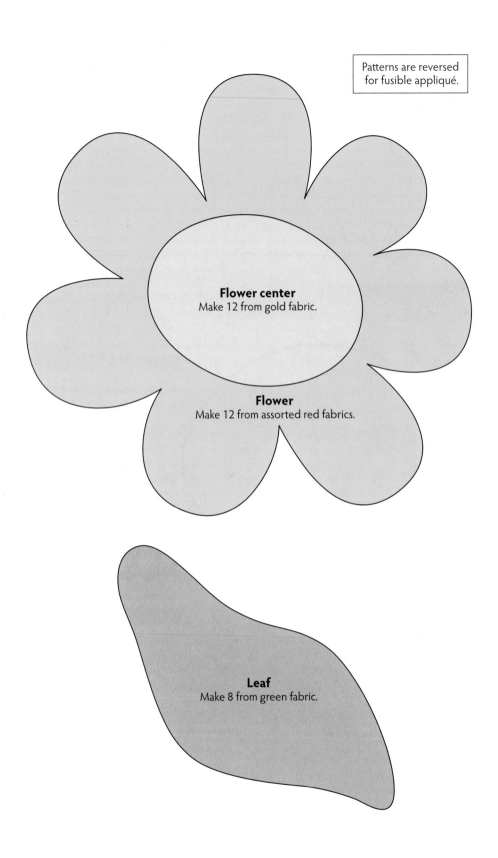

Patterns are reversed
for fusible appliqué.

Flower center
Make 12 from gold fabric.

Flower
Make 12 from assorted red fabrics.

Leaf
Make 8 from green fabric.

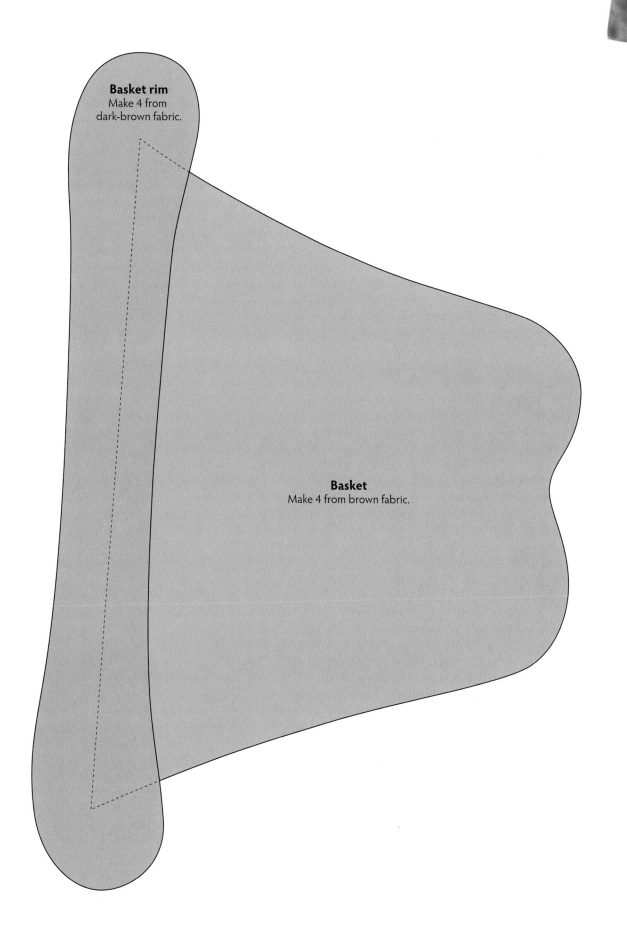

Basket rim
Make 4 from
dark-brown fabric.

Basket
Make 4 from brown fabric.

OAK AND ROSE

FINISHED QUILT: 63½" x 63½" ❄ **FINISHED BLOCK: 15" x 15"**

This quilt combines a vintage look with modern country colors. To make it look truly like "Grandma's old quilt," try using a variety of colors instead of the red.

Designed and pieced by Jeanne Large and Shelley Wicks; machine quilted by Laila Nelson

MATERIALS

Yardage is based on 42"-wide fabrics.

11 fat quarters (18" x 21") of assorted beige fabrics for blocks
2⅜ yards of dark-brown fabric for blocks, sashing, border, and binding
8 fat quarters of assorted red fabrics for blocks
4⅓ yards of fabric for backing
72" x 72" piece of batting

CUTTING

Cut all strips across the width of the fabric unless otherwise specified.

From *each* of 3 of the assorted beige fat quarters, cut:
3 strips, 3⅞" x 21" (9 total); crosscut into 12 squares, 3⅞" x 3⅞" (36 total). Cut each square in half diagonally to yield 24 triangles (72 total).
1 strip, 1½" x 21" (3 total)

From *each* of the 8 remaining beige fat quarters, cut:
10 strips, 1½" x 21" (80 total)

From the 8 assorted red fat quarters, cut a *total* of:
73 strips, 1½" x 21"

From the dark-brown fabric, cut:
4 strips, 3½" x 42"; crosscut into 36 squares, 3½" x 3½"
4 strips, 3⅞" x 42"; crosscut into 36 squares, 3⅞" x 3⅞". Cut each square in half diagonally to yield 72 triangles.
3 strips, 3½" x 42"; crosscut into 12 rectangles, 3½" x 9½"
3 strips, 6½" x 42"; crosscut into 12 rectangles, 6½" x 9½"
7 strips, 2½" x 42"

PIECING THE BLOCKS

1. Sew a beige 1½" x 21" strip to each long side of a red 1½" x 21" strip to make a strip set. Press the seam allowances toward the red strip. Repeat to make a total of 20 strip sets. Crosscut the strip sets into 100 rail-fence segments, 3½" wide.

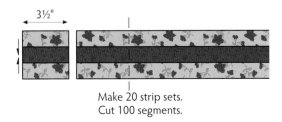

Make 20 strip sets.
Cut 100 segments.

2. Sew a red 1½" x 21" strip to each long side of a beige 1½" x 21" strip to make a strip set. Press the seam allowances toward the red strips. Repeat to make a total of 21 strip sets. Crosscut the strip sets into 250 segments, 1½" wide.

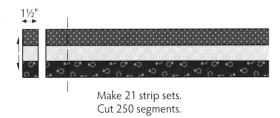

Make 21 strip sets.
Cut 250 segments.

3. Sew a beige 1½" x 21" strip to each long side of a red 1½" x 21" strip to make a strip set. Press the seam allowances toward the red strip. Repeat to make a total of 11 strip sets. Crosscut the strip sets into 125 segments, 1½" wide.

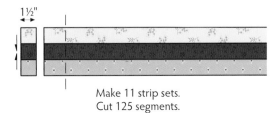

Make 11 strip sets.
Cut 125 segments.

4. Sew a segment from step 2 to each side of a segment from step 3 to make a nine-patch unit as shown. Press the seam allowances away from the center segment. Repeat to make a total of 125 nine-patch units.

Make 125.

5. Sew a beige 3⅞" triangle to a dark-brown 3⅞" triangle along the long edges as shown. Press the seam allowances toward the dark-brown triangle. Repeat to make a total of 72 half-square-triangle units.

Make 72.

6. Arrange four rail-fence segments from step 1, nine nine-patch units from step 4, eight half-square-triangle units from step 5, and four dark-brown 3½" squares into five horizontal rows as shown. Sew the pieces in each row together. Press the seam allowances as indicated. Sew the rows together. Press the seam allowances in one direction. Repeat to make a total of nine blocks. Set aside the remaining rail-fence segments and nine-patch units for the sashing and borders.

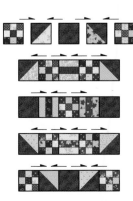
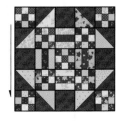

Make 9.

ASSEMBLING THE QUILT TOP

1. Sew a rail-fence segment to each end of a dark-brown 3½" x 9½" rectangle as shown. Press the seam allowances toward the rail-fence segments. Repeat to make a total of 12 sashing strips.

Make 12.

2. Alternately arrange three blocks and two sashing strips as shown to make a block row. Press the seam allowances toward the sashing strips. Repeat to make a total of three rows.

Make 3.

3. Sew a nine-patch unit to each end of a sashing strip. Press the seam allowances toward the sashing strip. Add a sashing strip to each end of this unit as shown. Press the seam allowances toward the sashing strips. Repeat to make a total of two sashing rows.

Make 2.

4. Alternately sew the block rows and sashing rows together as shown. Press the seam allowances toward the sashing rows.

5. Sew a rail-fence segment to a nine-patch unit as shown. Press the seam allowances toward the rail-fence unit. Repeat to make a total of 40 units.

Make 40.

6. Sew a unit from step 5 to each end of a dark-brown 6½" x 9½" rectangle as shown. Press the seam allowances toward the rectangle. Repeat to make a total of 12 border units.

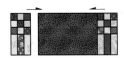

Make 12.

7. Alternately sew together three border segments and two units from step 5 as shown. Be careful to alternate the direction of the units from step 5 so that the pattern is created. Press the seam allowances in one direction. Repeat to make a total of four border strips. Refer to the quilt

Oak and Rose

assembly diagram below to sew border strips to opposite sides of the quilt top. Press the seam allowances toward the border strips.

Make 4.

8. Sew two units from step 5 together as shown to make a border corner block. Press the seam allowances as indicated. Repeat to make a total of two blocks. Make two additional blocks, arranging the units from step 5 as shown.

Make 2.   Make 2.

9. Refer to the quilt assembly diagram to sew the blocks to the ends of the remaining two border strips, making sure the nine-patch units alternate with the border nine-patch units. Press the seam allowances toward the border. Sew these borders to the top and bottom of the quilt top. Press the seam allowances toward the border.

Quilt assembly

FINISHING THE QUILT

Refer to "Finishing Basics" on page 16 for detailed instructions as needed.

1. Layer the backing, batting, and quilt top; baste.
2. Quilt as desired. Our quilt is machine quilted with an allover design.
3. Bind the quilt using the dark-brown 2½"-wide strips.

JEANNE'S MOST EXCELLENT CHOCOLATE CHIP COOKIES

1½ cups margarine
3 cups brown sugar, packed
3 eggs
3 tablespoons milk
1½ teaspoons baking soda
1½ teaspoons baking powder
3 cups flour
3 cups granola
3 cups semi-sweet chocolate chips

In a large bowl, cream together the margarine and brown sugar. Add the eggs and milk to the creamed mixture and mix well. In a smaller bowl, mix together the baking soda, baking powder, and flour. Add the dry ingredients to the creamed mixture and mix thoroughly. Stir in the granola and chocolate chips. Drop by rounded tablespoons 3" apart on an ungreased cookie sheet. Bake in a 350° oven for 8 to 10 minutes or until edges are browned. Transfer to a wire rack and let cool. Yields 24 large cookies.

Oak and Rose

ON A PRAIRIE CORNER

FINISHED QUILT: 48½" x 54½"

When we were kids, a drive in the country was always a treat. The landscape would change with the seasons, but our favorite was early fall with the crops slowly changing colors and the ditches full of wildflowers called brown-eyed Susans.

Designed and made by Jeanne Large and Shelley Wicks; machine quilted by Wendy Findlay

MATERIALS

Yardage is based on 42"-wide fabrics.

10 fat quarters (18" x 21") of assorted medium-beige fabrics for blocks

1 yard of dark-beige print for blocks

⅞ yard of dark-brown print for inner border and binding

½ yard of green print for stem and leaf appliqués

¼ yard of brown print for basket and handle appliqués

1 fat quarter of dark-gold print for large sunflower appliqués

1 fat quarter of medium-gold print fabric for large sunflower appliqués

1 fat quarter of dark-gold print fabric for daisy appliqués

7" x 13" rectangle of black tone-on-tone print for flower-center appliqués

3¼ yards of fabric for backing

57" x 63" piece of batting

1⅞ yards of 18"-wide lightweight paper-backed fusible web

Matching threads for appliqué

CUTTING

Cut all strips across the width of the fabric unless otherwise specified.

From the dark-beige print, cut:

5 strips, 3½" x 42"; crosscut into 45 squares, 3½" x 3½"

3 strips, 3½" x 42"; crosscut into 6 strips, 3½" x 21"

From *each* of the 10 assorted medium-beige fat quarters, cut:

1 strip, 6½" x 21" (10 total); crosscut into 5 rectangles, 3½" x 6½" (50 total; you'll have 5 left over)

2 strips, 3½" x 21" (20 total; you'll have 1 left over); crosscut *each of 13 strips* into 5 squares, 3½" x 3½" (65 total; you'll have 1 left over)

From the dark-brown print, cut:

5 strips, 2" x 42"

6 strips, 2½" x 42"

PIECING THE PANELS

1. Sew a dark-beige 3½" square to one end of a medium-beige 3½" x 6½" rectangle. Press the seam allowances toward the square. Repeat to make a total of 45 units.

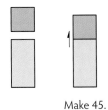

Make 45.

2. Sew 15 units from step 1 together along the long edges, alternating the direction of every other unit as shown. Press the seam allowances in one direction. The strip should measure 45½" long. Repeat to make a total of three wide panels.

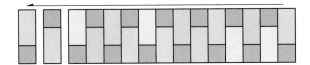

Make 3.

3. Join a medium-beige 3½" x 21" strip to a dark-beige 3½" x 21" strip along the long edges to make a strip set. Press the seam allowances

toward the dark-beige strip. Repeat to make a total of six strip sets. Crosscut the strip sets into 30 segments, 3½" wide.

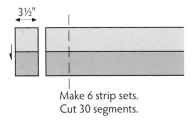

Make 6 strip sets.
Cut 30 segments.

4. Sew 15 segments from step 3 together along the long edges, alternating the direction of every other unit as shown. Press the seam allowances in the opposite direction of the wide panels. The strip should measure 45½" long. Repeat to make a total of two narrow panels.

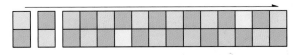

Make 2.

ASSEMBLING THE QUILT TOP

1. Refer to the quilt assembly diagram on page 44 to alternately arrange the wide and narrow panels in vertical rows, making sure the colors alternate across the quilt. Sew the panels together along the long edges. Press the seam allowances toward the narrow panels. The quilt center should now measure 39½" x 45½".

2. Sew the dark-brown 2" x 42" inner-border strips together end to end to make one long strip. From this strip, cut two strips, 2" x 45½", and two strips, 2" x 42½". Sew the 2" x 45½" strips to the sides of the quilt center. Press the seam allowances toward the inner border. Sew the 2" x 42½" strips to the top and bottom of the quilt center. Press the seam allowances toward the inner border.

SECURE THE BORDERS

It's helpful to backstitch at the beginning and end of the inner-border seams so they hold securely while doing the appliqué.

3. Refer to "Fusible-Web Appliqué" on page 12 and use the patterns on pages 45–49 to prepare the appliqués from the fabrics indicated. Refer to "Bias Vines" on page 14 for detailed instructions to prepare approximately 110" of bias stem from the green print.

4. Using the photo on page 42 as a guide, pin the bias stems in place. Arrange the appliqué shapes on the quilt top and press in place. Use matching thread to blanket-stitch around each shape by hand or machine.

5. Join 16 medium-beige squares end to end to make an outer-border strip. Press the seam allowances in one direction. Repeat to make a total of four strips. Sew border strips to opposite sides of the quilt top. Press the seam allowances toward the outer border. Sew the remaining border strips to the top and bottom of the quilt top. Press the seam allowances toward the outer border.

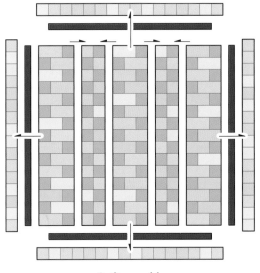

Quilt assembly

FINISHING THE QUILT

Refer to "Finishing Basics" on page 16 for detailed instructions as needed.

1. Layer the backing, batting, and quilt top; baste.

2. Quilt as desired. Our quilt is machine quilted with an allover design.

3. Bind the quilt using the dark-brown 2½"-wide strips.

Daisy
Make 6 from
dark-gold print.

Daisy center
Make 6 from black
tone-on-tone print.

Leaf
Make 12 from green print.

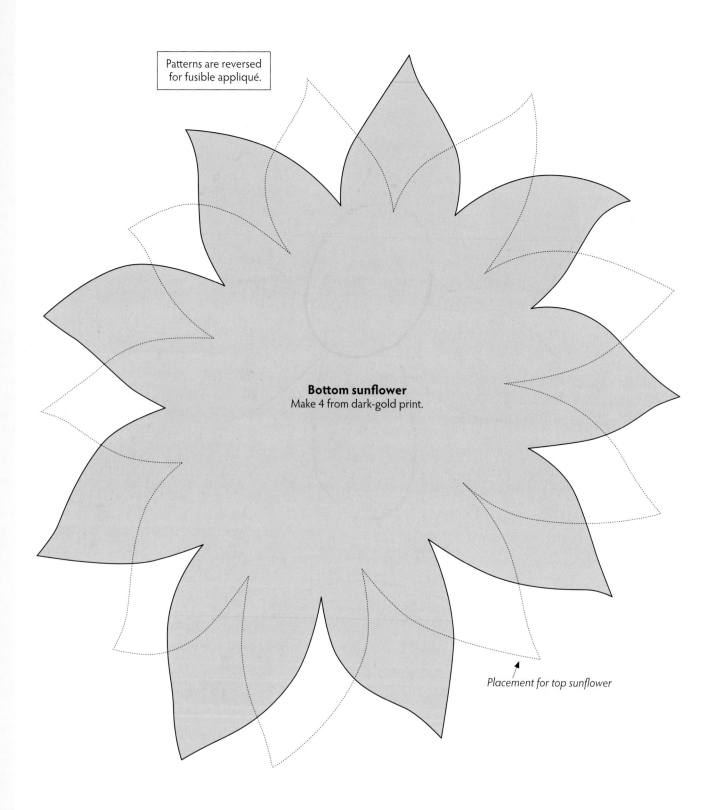

Patterns are reversed
for fusible appliqué.

Bottom sunflower
Make 4 from dark-gold print.

Placement for top sunflower

On a Prairie Corner

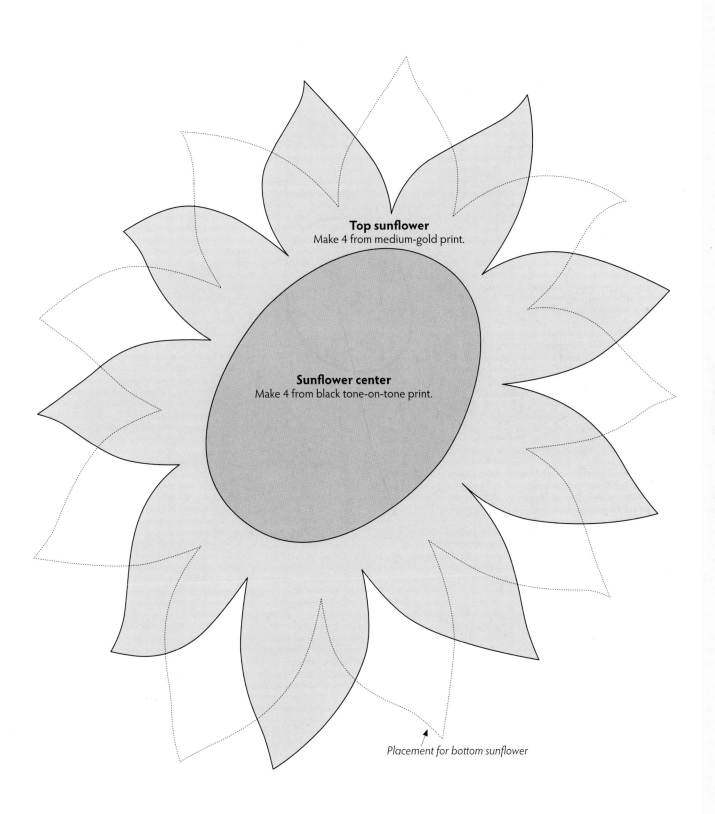

Top sunflower
Make 4 from medium-gold print.

Sunflower center
Make 4 from black tone-on-tone print.

Placement for bottom sunflower

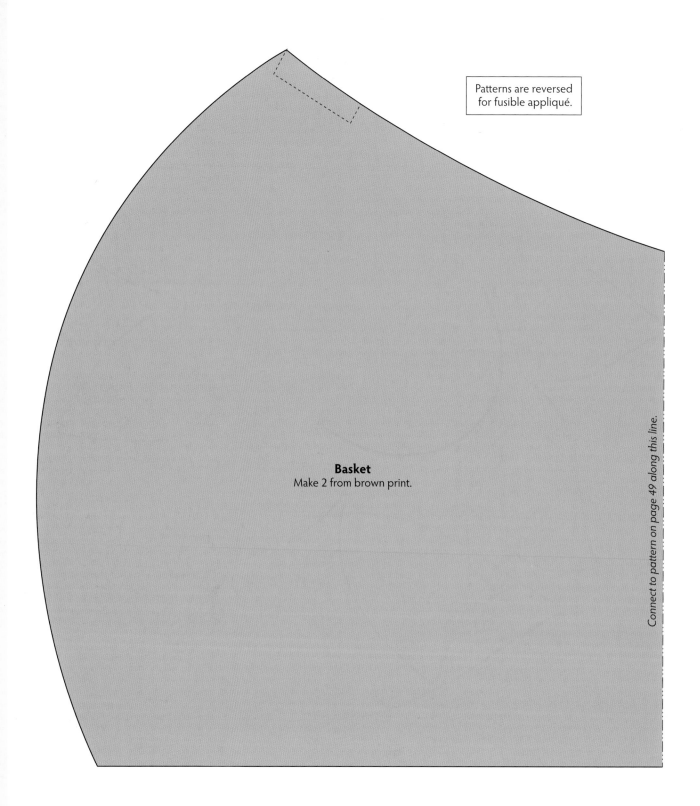

Basket
Make 2 from brown print.

Patterns are reversed
for fusible appliqué.

Connect to pattern on page 49 along this line.

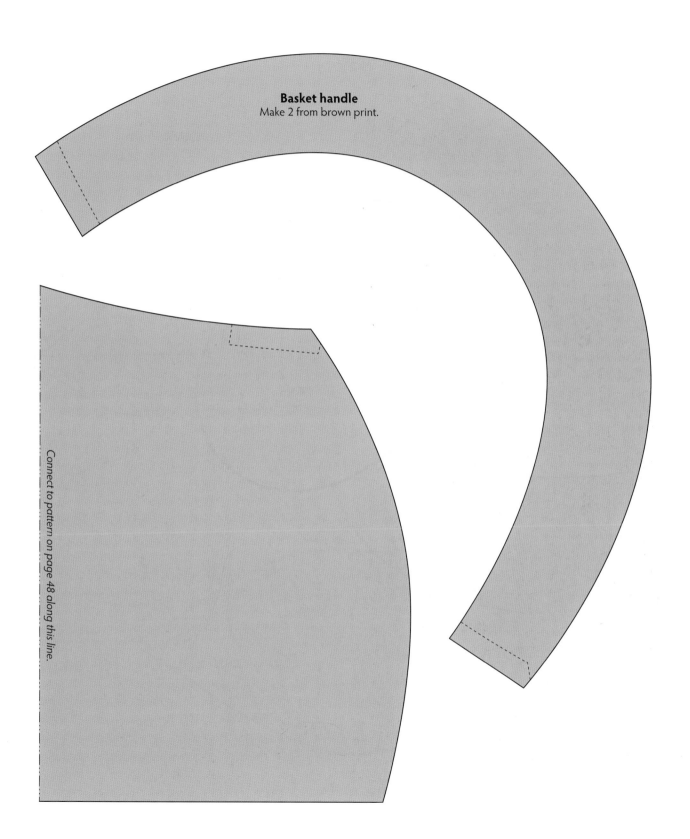

Basket handle
Make 2 from brown print.

Connect to pattern on page 48 along this line.

JO'S JAMMIES

FINISHED QUILT: 64½" x 78½" ❀ **FINISHED BLOCK: 9½" x 9½"**

Some quilts just make you want to curl up in your pajamas with a good book and a bowl of popcorn. The warm colors in this quilt make it the perfect choice to cuddle up with.

Designed and pieced by Jeanne Large and Shelley Wicks; machine quilted by Wendy Findlay

MATERIALS

Yardage is based on 42"-wide fabrics.

6 fat quarters (18" x 21") of assorted gold fabrics for Star blocks and pieced second border

3 fat quarters *each* of assorted dark-red and assorted green fabrics for Star block backgrounds and pieced second border

1⅓ yards of black tone-on-tone print for first and third borders and binding

1¼ yards of dark-red print for outer border

1 fat quarter *each* of dark-red, green, and dark-gold, and two assorted rust fabrics for side setting triangles and pieced second border

1 fat quarter *each* of green, brown, and dark-red fabrics for alternate blocks

1 fat quarter of dark-brown for Star blocks

1 fat quarter of green fabric for corner setting triangles

4¾ yards of fabric for backing

73" x 87" piece of batting

CUTTING

Cut all strips across the width of the fabric unless otherwise specified.

From *each* of the 6 assorted gold fat quarters, cut:

1 strip, 3½" x 21" (6 total); crosscut into 2 squares, 3½" x 3½" (12 total)

1 strip, 4¼" x 21" (6 total); crosscut into 4 squares, 4¼" x 4¼" (24 total). Cut each square into quarters diagonally to yield 16 triangles (96 total).

3 strips, 2½" x 21" (18 total)

From the dark-brown fat quarter, cut:

3 strips, 4¼" x 21"; crosscut into 12 squares, 4¼" x 4¼". Cut each square into quarters diagonally to yield 48 triangles.

From *each* of the 3 assorted dark-red and 3 assorted green fat quarters, cut:

2 strips, 3½" x 21" (12 total); crosscut into 8 squares, 3½" x 3½" (48 total)

1 strip, 4¼" x 21" (6 total); crosscut into 2 squares, 4¼" x 4¼" (12 total). Cut each square into quarters diagonally to yield 8 triangles (48 total).

2 strips, 2½" x 21" (12 total)

From *each* of the green, brown, and dark-red fat quarters for alternate blocks, cut:

1 strip, 9½" x 21" (3 total); crosscut into 2 squares, 9½" x 9½" (6 total)

2 strips, 2½" x 21" (6 total)

From *each* of the 5 assorted dark-red, green, dark-gold, and rust fat quarters for side setting triangles, cut:

1 strip, 10½" x 21" (5 total); crosscut into 1 square, 10½" x 10½" (5 total). Cut each square in half diagonally to yield 2 triangles (10 total).

2 strips, 2½" x 21" (10 total)

From the green fat quarter for corner setting triangles, cut:

1 strip, 8½" x 21"; crosscut into 2 squares, 8½" x 8½". Cut each square in half diagonally to yield 4 triangles.

3 strips, 2½" x 21"

From the black tone-on-tone print, cut:

3 strips, 2" x 42"

10 strips, 1½" x 42"

8 strips, 2½" x 42"

From the dark-red print, cut:

7 strips, 5½" x 42"

PIECING THE BLOCKS

1. Arrange two matching gold triangles, one dark-brown triangle, and one of the green or red Star block background triangles as shown. Sew the triangles into pairs. Press the seam allowances toward the gold triangles. Sew the pairs together to make an hourglass unit. Press the seam allowances in one direction. Repeat to make four matching hourglass units.

Make 4 matching units.

2. Arrange four hourglass units from step 1, four matching green or red 3½" background squares, and one matching gold 3½" square into three horizontal rows as shown. Sew the pieces in each row together. Pressing the seam allowances toward the squares. Sew the rows together. Press the seam allowances toward the top and bottom rows.

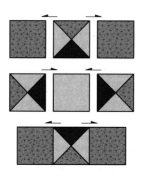 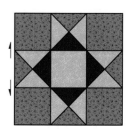

Make 12.

3. Repeat steps 1 and 2 to make a total of 12 Star blocks.

Jo's Jammies

ASSEMBLING THE QUILT TOP

1. Refer to the illustration below to arrange the Star blocks; the green, brown, and dark-red 9½" square alternate blocks; the dark-red, green, dark-gold, and assorted rust 10½" side setting triangles; and green corner setting triangles into diagonal rows as shown. Sew the blocks and side setting triangles in each row together. Press the seam allowances toward the alternate blocks and side setting triangles. Sew the rows together. Press the seam allowances away from the center row. Add the corner triangles last. Press the seam allowances toward the corner triangles.

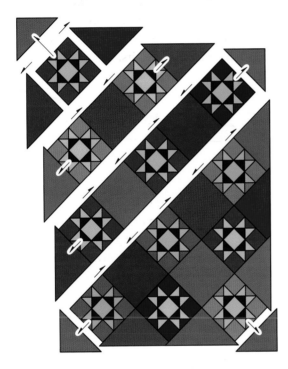

2. Trim around the outside edge of the quilt, ¼" from the block points to remove the excess setting triangle fabric. Your quilt center must measure 38½" x 51½" in order for the pieced second border to fit.

3. Sew three of the black 1½" x 42" first-border strips together end to end to make one long strip. From this strip, cut two strips, 1½" x 51½". Sew these strips to the sides of the quilt top. Press the seam allowances toward the first border. Sew the black 2" x 42" first-border strips together end to end to make one long strip. From this strip, cut

two strips, 2" x 40½". Sew these strips to the top and bottom of the quilt top. Press the seam allowances toward the first border.

4. To make the pieced second border, randomly select three 2½" x 21" strips and sew them together along the long edges to make a strip set. Press the seam allowances in one direction. Repeat to make a total of 16 strips sets. You'll have one 2½" x 21" strip left over. Crosscut the strip sets into 106 segments, 2½" wide.

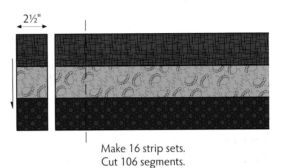

2½"

Make 16 strip sets.
Cut 106 segments.

5. Refer to the quilt assembly diagram on page 54 to randomly sew 27 segments from step 4 together along the long edges. Press the seam allowances in one direction. Repeat to make a total of two second-border strips. Sew these strips to the sides of the quilt top. Press the seam allowances toward the first border. In the same manner, join 26 segments from step 4 along the long edges and press the seam allowances in one direction. Repeat to make a total of two second-border strips. Sew these strips to the top and bottom of the quilt top. Press the seam allowances toward the first border.

6. Sew the remaining black 1½" x 42" third-border strips together end to end to make one long strip. From this strip, cut two strips, 1½" x 66½", and two strips, 1½" x 54½". Sew the 1½" x 66½" strips to the sides of the quilt top. Press the seam allowances toward the third border. Sew the 1½" x 54½" strips to the top and bottom of the quilt top. Press the seam allowances toward the third border.

7. Sew the dark-red 5½" x 42" fourth-border strips together end to end to make one long strip. From this strip, cut two strips, 5½" x 68½", and two strips, 5½" x 64½". Sew the 5½" x 68½" strips to the sides of the quilt top. Press the seam allowances toward the fourth border. Sew the 5½" x 64½" strips to the top and bottom of the quilt top. Press the seam allowances toward the fourth border.

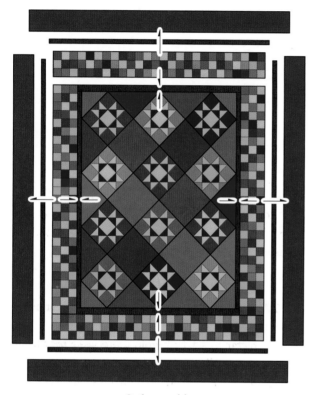

Quilt assembly

FINISHING THE QUILT

Refer to "Finishing Basics" on page 16 for detailed instructions as needed.

1. Layer the backing, batting, and quilt top; baste.
2. Quilt as desired. Our quilt is machine quilted with an allover design.
3. Bind the quilt using the black 2½"-wide strips.

JO'S POPPYCOCK

1 cup salted peanuts
1 cup slivered almonds
1 cup pecans
8 cups popped popcorn
1 cup margarine
1½ cups white sugar
½ cup light corn syrup
½ teaspoon cream of tartar
½ teaspoon baking soda
½ teaspoon vanilla

Mix the peanuts, almonds, and pecans together in a large roasting pan. Toast in a 300° oven for 10 minutes. Add the popcorn to the toasted nuts.

Grease two cookie sheets. In a medium saucepan, melt the margarine. Stir in the sugar, corn syrup, and cream of tartar. Bring to a boil and boil for 6 to 8 minutes until foamy. Remove from heat and stir in the baking soda and vanilla. The mixture will foam when you add the baking soda. Pour the mixture over the popcorn and nuts and stir quickly. Pour the mixture onto the greased cookie sheets and press down firmly. Let the mixture cool completely, then break up and store in airtight containers.

Jo's Jammies

PEPPER CREEK

FINISHED QUILT: 32½" x 32½" ❈ **FINISHED BLOCK: 16" x 16"**

This piece makes a great table topper or wall hanging, or you could even take it to a framing shop to have it mounted and framed. Wherever you use this quilt, the dark, rich colors of wool will be admired.

Designed and made by Jeanne Large and Shelley Wicks

MATERIALS

Yardage is based on 42"-wide fabrics.

1⅜ yards of black flannel for block background
   and binding
16" x 25" rectangle of green felted wool for stem,
   leaf, and center-circle appliqués
12" x 18" rectangle of red felted wool #1 for flower
   A and B appliqués
4" x 12" rectangle of brown felted wool #1 for flower
   A center appliqués
4" x 20" rectangle of dark-gold felted wool for flower
   B crown appliqués
3" x 12" rectangle of gold felted wool #1 for flower
   B center appliqués
9" x 9" square of red felted wool #2 for flower
   C appliqués
4" x 5" rectangle of brown felted wool #2 for flower
   C center appliqués
8" x 22" rectangle of gold felted wool #2 for flower
   D appliqués
5" x 12" rectangle of dark-red felted wool for flower
   D center appliqués
1⅓ yards of fabric for backing
40" x 40" piece of batting
1⅞ yards of 18"-wide lightweight paper-backed
   fusible web
Matching threads for appliqué

CUTTING

Cut all strips across the width of the fabric unless otherwise specified.

From the fusible web, cut:
1 rectangle, 6" x 25"

From the green felted wool, cut:
1 rectangle, 6" x 25"

From the black flannel, cut:
2 strips, 16½" x 42"; crosscut into 4 squares, 16½" x 16½"
4 strips, 2½" x 42"

APPLIQUÉING THE BLOCKS

1. Refer to "Wool Appliqué" on page 13 and follow the manufacturer's instructions to fuse the 6" x 25" fusible-web rectangle to the green wool 6" x 25" rectangle. From the fused piece, cut 10 strips, ½" x 25". The narrow strips will be easy to manipulate into the shape you desire.

2. Refer to "Wool Appliqué" and use the patterns on pages 58 and 59 to prepare the appliqués from the fabrics indicated.

3. Using the appliqué placement diagram below and the photo, opposite, as guides, cut the green wool ½" x 25" strips to the lengths desired for the stems and pin them in place on the flannel square. Arrange all of the appliqué shapes, except for the C flowers and C flower centers, and press in place. Use matching thread to blanket-stitch around each shape by hand or machine. Repeat to make a total of four blocks. Note that you'll use approximately two and one half stem strips per square.

Appliqué placement.
Leave off flower C on all blocks until the blocks are joined.

ASSEMBLING THE TABLE TOPPER

1. Arrange the blocks in two rows of two blocks each, rotating the blocks so all the long stems point toward the center. Sew the blocks in each row together. Press the seam allowances in opposite directions in each row. Join the rows to form the table topper. Press the seam allowances in one direction.

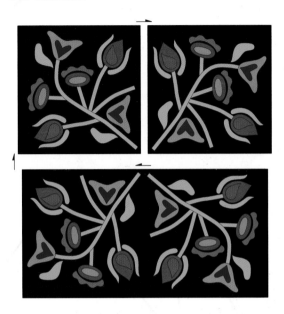

2. Arrange the C flowers, C flower centers, and center circle appliqués on the table topper and press in place. Use matching thread to blanket-stitch around each shape by hand or machine.

FINISHING THE TABLE TOPPER

Refer to "Finishing Basics" on page 16 for detailed instructions as needed.

1. Layer the backing, batting, and quilt top; baste.
2. Quilt as desired. Our table topper is machine quilted in an allover design.
3. Bind the quilt using the black flannel 2½"-wide strips.

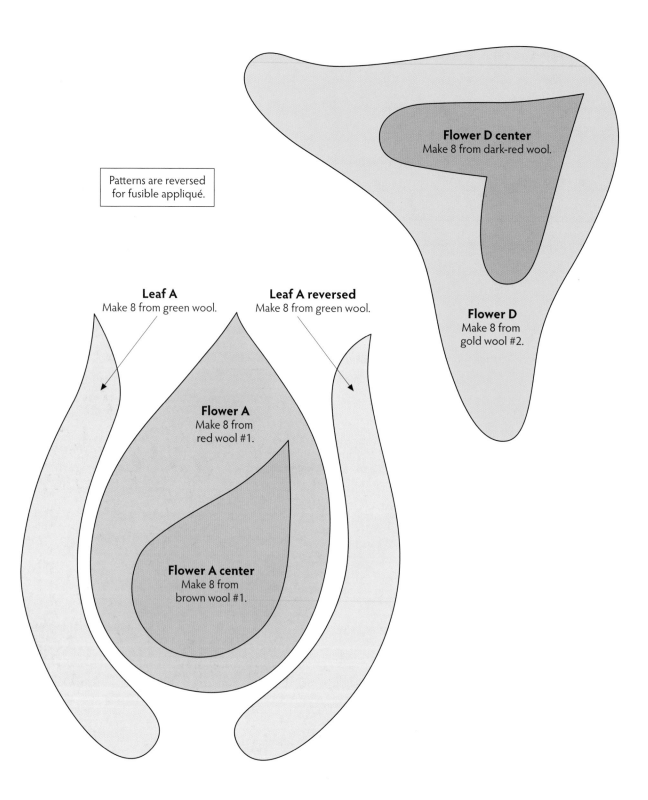

Flower D center
Make 8 from dark-red wool.

Flower D
Make 8 from
gold wool #2.

Patterns are reversed
for fusible appliqué.

Leaf A
Make 8 from green wool.

Leaf A reversed
Make 8 from green wool.

Flower A
Make 8 from
red wool #1.

Flower A center
Make 8 from
brown wool #1.

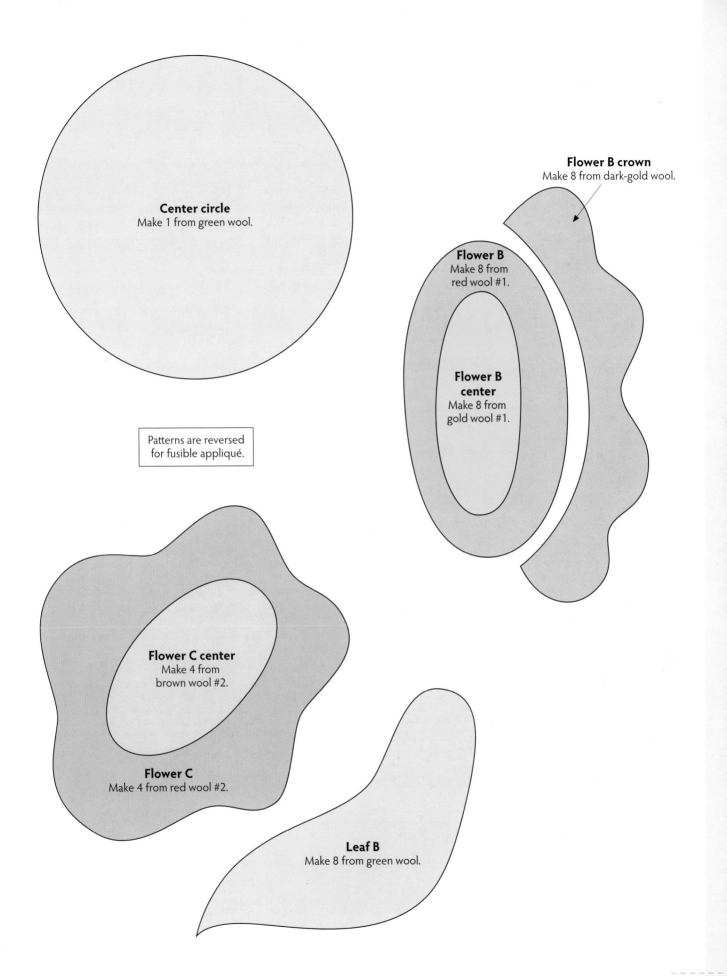

Center circle
Make 1 from green wool.

Flower B crown
Make 8 from dark-gold wool.

Flower B
Make 8 from
red wool #1.

**Flower B
center**
Make 8 from
gold wool #1.

Patterns are reversed
for fusible appliqué.

Flower C center
Make 4 from
brown wool #2.

Flower C
Make 4 from red wool #2.

Leaf B
Make 8 from green wool.

SWEET POTATO PIE

Where we come from, it's common to see fields of sunflowers with their heads nodding in the sun, changing direction as it moves across the sky. It's a familiar sight, but one that never fails to take your breath away with its natural beauty. We hope this lap quilt and matching pillow bring sunshine into your home and create memories as sweet as sweet potato pie.

Designed and pieced by Jeanne Large and Shelley Wicks; machine quilted by Wendy Findlay

SWEET POTATO PIE LAP QUILT

FINISHED QUILT: 60½" x 77½"
FINISHED BLOCK: 11½" x 11½"

MATERIALS

Yardage is based on 42"-wide fabrics.

4½ yards of black small-scale print for block backgrounds, appliquéd panel background, outer border, and binding

16 fat eighths (9" x 21") of assorted gold and rust fabrics for pieced blocks

3 fat quarters (18" x 21") of assorted gold fabrics for sunflower appliqués

⅜ yard of rust fabric for inner border

10" x 28" rectangle of black fabric for sunflower-center appliqués

13" x 21" rectangle of green fabric for leaf appliqués

1 fat eighth of dark-gold fabric for star appliqués

4¾ yards of fabric for backing

68" x 85" piece of batting

4⅔ yards of ⅝"-wide green rickrack for vines and stems

2 yards of 18"-wide lightweight paper-backed fusible web

Black thread for appliqué

CUTTING

Cut all strips across the width of the fabric unless otherwise specified.

From the black small-scale print, cut:

8 strips, 7" x 42"; crosscut into 36 squares, 7" x 7". Cut each square in half diagonally to yield 2 triangles (72 total).

8 strips, 2½" x 42"

From the *lengthwise grain* of the remainder of the black small-scale print, cut:

1 rectangle, 18" x 69½"

2 strips, 3½" x 71½"

2 strips, 3½" x 60½"

From *each* of the 16 assorted gold and rust fat eighths, cut:

3 strips, 2½" x 21" (48 total)

From the rust fabric, cut:

7 strips, 1½" x 42"

PIECING THE BLOCKS

1. Randomly sew four assorted 2½" x 21" strips together along the long edges to make a strip set. Press the seam allowances in one direction. Repeat to make a total of 12 strip sets. Crosscut the strip sets into 72 segments, 2½" wide.

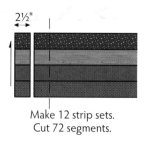

2½"

Make 12 strip sets.
Cut 72 segments.

2. Randomly sew four strip-set segments from step 1 together along the long edges, arranging segments so squares of the same color aren't side by side, and rotating the segments so the seam allowances alternate directions. Press the seam allowances in one direction. Repeat to make a total of 18 block-center units.

Make 18.

3. Center and sew black triangles to opposite sides of each block-center unit. The triangles are slightly longer than the blocks. Press the seam allowances toward the triangles. Repeat on the remaining sides of the block-center units. Square up each block to measure 12" x 12".

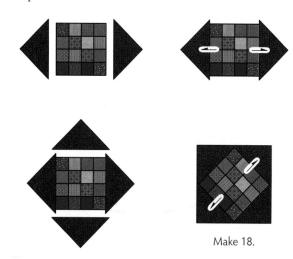

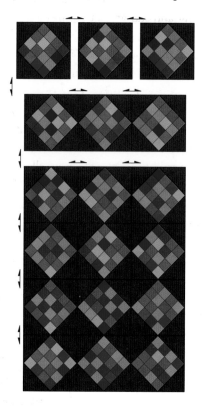

Make 18.

ASSEMBLING THE QUILT TOP

1. Arrange the blocks into six rows of three blocks each. Sew the blocks in each row together. Press the seam allowances open. Sew the rows together. Press the seam allowances open.

2. Refer to "Rickrack Stems and Vines" on page 15 and the photo on page 61 to arrange the rickrack on the black 18" x 69½" rectangle for the vines and stems. Sew the rickrack in place.

3. Refer to "Fusible-Web Appliqué" on page 12 and use the patterns on pages 66–68 and below to prepare the appliqués from the fabrics indicated.

4. Use the appliqué placement diagram below and the photo as guides to arrange the appliqué shapes on the black rectangle, leaving off the three flowers and two stars that overlap onto the pieced block section. Press them in place, being careful not to scorch the rickrack. Use black thread to blanket-stitch around each shape by hand or machine.

Appliqué placement

5. Sew the appliquéd panel to one long edge of the pieced block section as shown. Press the seam allowances toward the appliquéd panel.

6. Refer to the photo to arrange the remaining flower and star appliqués on the quilt top and press them in place. Use black thread to blanket-stitch around each shape by hand or machine.

7. Sew the rust 1½" x 42" inner-border strips together end to end to make one long strip. From the strip, cut two strips, 1½" x 69½", and two strips, 1½" x 54½". Refer to the quilt assembly diagram to sew the 1½" x 69½" strips to the sides of the quilt top. Press the seam allowances toward the inner border. Sew the 1½" x 54½" strips to the top and bottom of the quilt top. Press the seam allowances toward the inner border.

8. Sew the black 3½" x 71½" outer-border strips to the sides of the quilt top. Press the seam allowances toward the outer border. Sew the black 3½" x 60½" outer-border strips to the top and bottom of the quilt top. Press the seam allowances toward the outer border.

> Pattern is reversed for fusible appliqué.
>
> Additional appliqué patterns are on pages 66-68.

FINISHING THE QUILT

Refer to "Finishing Basics" on page 16 for detailed instructions as needed.

1. Layer the backing, batting, and quilt top; baste.
2. Quilt as desired. Our quilt is machine quilted with an allover design.
3. Bind the quilt using the black 2½"-wide strips.

Quilt assembly

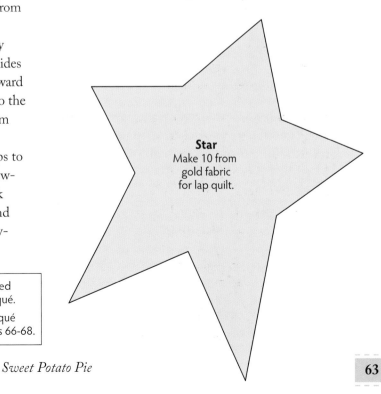

Star
Make 10 from gold fabric for lap quilt.

Sweet Potato Pie

Designed and made by Jeanne Large and Shelley Wicks

SWEET POTATO PIE PILLOW

FINISHED PILLOW: 18½" x 38½"

MATERIALS

Yardage is based on 42"-wide fabrics.

4 fat eighths (9" x 21") of assorted black fabrics
   for appliqué background
4 fat eighths of assorted gold and rust fabrics
   for pieced border
6½" x 23" rectangle of gold fabric #1 for
   sunflower appliqués
6½" x 15½" rectangle of gold fabric #2 for
   sunflower appliqués
4" x 22" rectangle of black fabric for sunflower-
   center appliqués
5" x 15" rectangle of green fabric for leaf appliqués
1½ yards of muslin for pillow-top back
¼ yard of black fabric for binding
⅞ yard of fabric for backing
26" x 46" piece of batting
2 yards of ⅝"-wide green rickrack for vines
⅝ yard of 18"-wide lightweight paper-backed
   fusible web
Black thread for appliqué
18" x 38" pillow form

CUTTING

*Cut all strips across the width of the fabric unless
otherwise specified.*

From *each* of the 4 assorted black fat eighths, cut:
1 strip, 7½" x 21" (4 total); crosscut into 3 rectangles,
   5½" x 7½" (12 total)

**From *each* of the 4 assorted gold and rust
fabrics, cut:**
3 strips, 2½" x 21" (12 total)

From the muslin, cut:
1 rectangle, 26" x 46"

From the backing fabric, cut:
1 strip, 25" x 42"; crosscut into 2 rectangles,
   18½" x 25"

From the black fabric for binding, cut:
3 strips, 2½" x 42"

ASSEMBLING THE PILLOW TOP

1. Arrange the assorted black 5½" x 7½" rectangles
   into two rows of six rectangles each as shown.
   Sew the rectangles in each row together. Press
   the seam allowances in opposite directions in
   each row. Sew the rows together. Press the seam
   allowances in one direction. The pieced background should measure 30½" x 14½". Stay stitch

⅛" from the rectangle edges to keep the seams from unraveling while you appliqué.

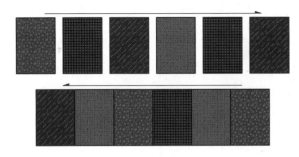

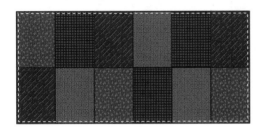

2. Refer to "Rickrack Stems and Vines" on page 15 and the photo on page 64 to arrange the rickrack on the pieced background for the vines. Sew the rickrack in place.

3. Refer to "Fusible-Web Appliqué" on page 12 and the "Appliqué Patterns" box below to prepare the appliqués listed:

From the green fabric, cut:
5 leaves

From the gold fabric #2, cut:
3 of sunflower C
2 of sunflower D

From the black fabric, cut:
3 of Sunflower C center
2 of Sunflower D center

APPLIQUÉ PATTERNS

You can either reduce the sunflower appliqué patterns on pages 67 and 68 by 80% or download the full-sized patterns online at www.shopmartingale.com/extras.

4. Using the appliqué placement diagram above right and the photo as guides, arrange the

appliqué shapes on the pieced background and press in place, being careful not to scorch the rickrack. Use black thread to blanket-stitch around each shape by hand or machine.

Appliqué placement

5. Sew two assorted rust or gold 2½" x 21" strips together along the long edges to make a strip set. Press the seam allowances in one direction. Repeat to make a total of six strip sets. Crosscut the strip sets into 33 segments, 2½" wide.

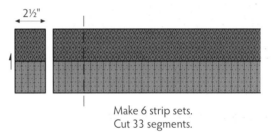

Make 6 strip sets.
Cut 33 segments.

6. To make the side borders, randomly sew seven strip-set segments together along the long edges, arranging segments so squares of the same color aren't side by side and rotating the segments so the seam allowances alternate directions. Press the seam allowances in one direction. Repeat to make a total of two border strips.

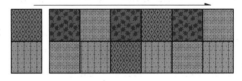

Make 2.

7. To make the top and bottom borders, randomly sew nine strip-set segments together along the short ends. Press the seam allowances in one direction. Repeat to make a total of two strips. Remove the seam from the remaining strip-set segment and sew a square to one end of each

strip. Press the seam allowances in the same direction as the other seam allowances of the strip.

Make 2.

8. Refer to the pillow assembly diagram below to sew the side borders to the sides of the pillow top. Press the seam allowances toward the pillow top. Sew the top and bottom borders to the top and bottom edges of the pillow top. Press the seam allowances toward the pillow top.

Pillow assembly

FINISHING THE PILLOW

Refer to "Finishing Basics" on page 16 for detailed instructions as needed.

1. Layer the muslin backing rectangle, batting, and pillow top; baste.
2. Quilt as desired. Our pillow is custom quilted.
3. To make the pillow backing, turn under ½" of one short side of each backing rectangle. Stitch ¼" from the fold. Lay the backing pieces under the pillow top, *wrong* sides together and outer edges even; the hemmed edges will overlap in the center of the pillow. Sew all around the outer edges of the pillow using a ¼" seam allowance.

4. Bind the pillow using the black 2½"-wide strips. Insert the pillow form through the opening in the back.

EDNA'S PUMPKIN PIE

2 eggs, slightly beaten
2 cups cooked and pureed fresh pumpkin, or canned pumpkin
¾ cup brown sugar
½ teaspoon salt
1 teaspoon cinnamon
½ teaspoon ginger
¼ teaspoon cloves
¼ teaspoon nutmeg
1½ cups light cream
9" pie shell

Mix all ingredients together in a large bowl. Pour mixture into pie shell. Bake at 450° for 10 minutes, then lower heat to 350° and bake for 35 to 40 minutes longer or until filling is set and a knife inserted in the center comes out clean.

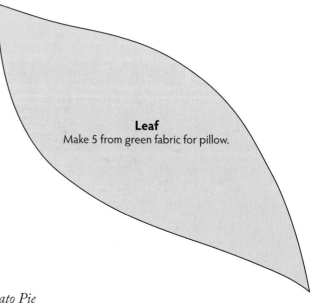

Leaf
Make 5 from green fabric for pillow.

Sweet Potato Pie

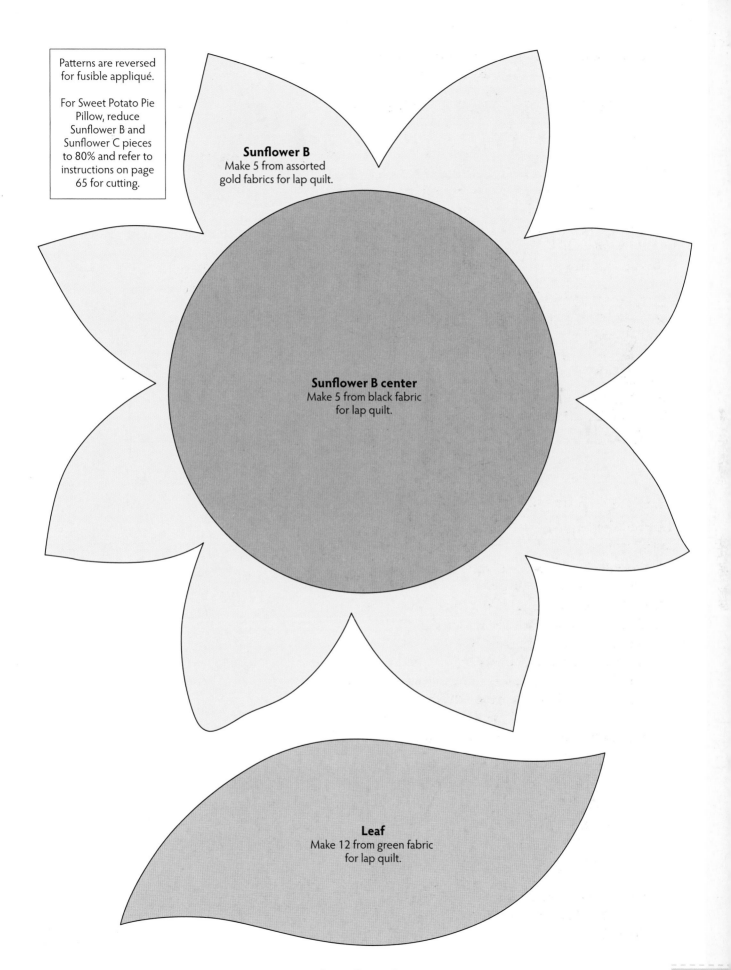

Patterns are reversed for fusible appliqué.

For Sweet Potato Pie Pillow, reduce Sunflower B and Sunflower C pieces to 80% and refer to instructions on page 65 for cutting.

Sunflower B
Make 5 from assorted gold fabrics for lap quilt.

Sunflower B center
Make 5 from black fabric for lap quilt.

Leaf
Make 12 from green fabric for lap quilt.

Sweet Potato Pie

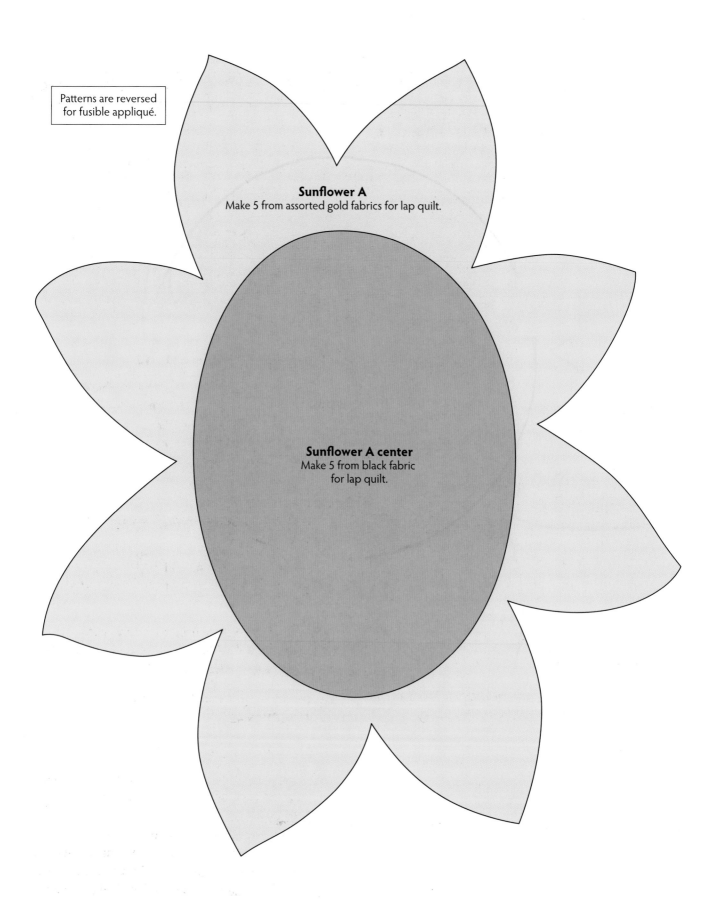

Patterns are reversed
for fusible appliqué.

Sunflower A
Make 5 from assorted gold fabrics for lap quilt.

Sunflower A center
Make 5 from black fabric
for lap quilt.

ZELDA

FINISHED QUILT: 56½" x 64½" ❋ **FINISHED BLOCK: 8" x 8"**

This fun quilt can be made in a variety of colors to match any decor. It can be as funky and modern or as traditional and subdued as you want it to be.

Designed and pieced by Jeanne Large and Shelley Wicks; machine quilted by Wendy Findlay

MATERIALS

Yardage is based on 42"-wide fabrics.

1 yard *each* of 4 assorted red prints for blocks
3⅞ yards of medium-beige print for blocks
⅝ yard of red print for binding
3¾ yards of fabric for backing
64" x 72" piece of batting

CUTTING

Cut all strips across the width of the fabric unless otherwise specified.

From the medium-beige print, cut:
28 strips, 4½" x 42"; crosscut into 224 squares, 4½" x 4½"

From *each* of the 4 assorted red prints, cut:
7 strips, 4½" x 42" (28 total); crosscut into 28 rectangles, 4½" x 8½" (112 total)

From the red print for binding, cut:
7 strips, 2½" x 42"

PIECING THE BLOCKS

1. Use a pencil and ruler to lightly draw a diagonal line on the wrong side of each medium-beige 4½" square.
2. Layer one of the marked squares over one end of an assorted red 4½" x 8½" rectangle as shown. Sew from corner to corner directly on the drawn line. Fold the top corner back and align it with

the corner of the rectangle beneath it; press. Trim away the excess layers of fabric beneath the top triangle, leaving a ¼" seam allowance. In the same manner, layer a marked square on the opposite end of the rectangle as shown and stitch, press, and trim to make an A unit. Repeat to make a total of 56 A units.

Unit A.
Make 56.

3. Repeat step 2 with the remaining marked squares and red rectangles, orienting the marked squares as shown, to make 56 B units.

Unit B.
Make 56.

4. Join an A unit to a B unit along the long edges as shown. Press the seam allowances open. Repeat to make a total of 56 blocks.

Unit A Unit B   Make 56.

ASSEMBLING THE QUILT TOP

Arrange the blocks into eight rows of seven blocks each as shown. Sew the blocks in each row together. Press the seam allowances open. Sew the rows together. Press the seam allowances open.

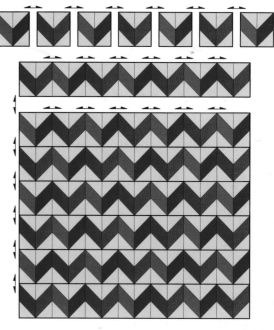

Quilt assembly

FINISHING THE QUILT

Refer to "Finishing Basics" on page 16 for detailed instructions as needed.

1. Layer the backing, batting, and quilt top; baste.
2. Quilt as desired. Our quilt is quilted with an all-over design.
3. Bind the quilt using the red 2½"-wide strips.

Zelda

CRANBERRY COTTAGE

This lap quilt and matching table runner look wonderful together. Arrange them in a family-room setting, with the quilt ready to be snuggled under and the runner marching along the coffee table. It's a sure way to perk up your surroundings.

Designed and pieced by Jeanne Large and Shelley Wicks; machine quilted by Wendy Findlay

CRANBERRY COTTAGE LAP QUILT

FINISHED QUILT: 70½" x 70½"

MATERIALS

Yardage is based on 42"-wide fabrics.

¼ yard *each* of 19 assorted red, pink, green, brown, and gold fabrics for center block and pieced fourth border

2 yards of black small-scale print for first border, third border, fifth border, and binding

1½ yards of gold fabric for appliquéd second border and third-border corner squares

½ yard of green fabric for bias vines and leaf appliqués

1 fat quarter (18" x 21") of light-green fabric for flower A large-center appliqués

13" x 14" rectangle *each* of 5 assorted red fabrics for flower A appliqués

10" x 17" rectangle of dark-green fabric for flower A small-center appliqués

10" x 13" rectangle of purple fabric for flower B appliqués

7" x 10" rectangle of medium-green for flower B base appliqués

7" x 9" rectangle of rust fabric for flower B center appliqués

2¾ yards of 18"-wide lightweight paper-backed fusible web

4⅓ yards of fabric for backing

78" x 78" piece of batting

Matching threads for appliqué

CUTTING

Cut all strips across the width of the fabric unless otherwise specified.

From *each* of the 19 assorted red, pink, green, brown, and gold fabrics, cut:

2 strips, 3" x 42" (38 total; you'll have 1 extra)

From the black small-scale print, cut:

9 strips, 2" x 42"; crosscut *4 of the strips* into:
    2 strips, 2" x 25½"
    2 strips, 2" x 28½"
7 strips, 3½" x 42"
8 strips, 2½" x 42"

From the *lengthwise grain* of the gold fabric, cut:

4 strips, 10" x 49"; crosscut the strips into:
    2 strips, 10" x 47½"
    2 strips, 10" x 28½"
    4 squares, 7½" x 7½"

PIECING THE CENTER SQUARE

1. Randomly sew three assorted 3" x 42" strips together along the long edges to make a strip set. Press the seam allowances in one direction. Repeat to make a total of 8 strip sets. Crosscut the strips sets into 97 segments, 3" wide.

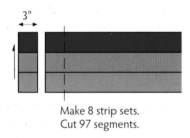

Make 8 strip sets.
Cut 97 segments.

2. Randomly sew two assorted 3" x 42" strips together along the long edges to make a strip set. Press the seam allowances in one direction. Repeat to make a total of six strip sets. Crosscut the strip sets into 72 segments, 3" wide.

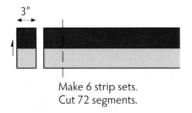

Make 6 strip sets.
Cut 72 segments.

3. Crosscut the remaining assorted 3" x 42" strip into 10 squares, 3" x 3".

4. Arrange 29 strip-set segments from step 1, 12 strip-set segments from step 2, and two 3" squares from step 3 into diagonal rows as shown, rotating the pieces so that the seam allowances alternate from row to row. Sew the pieces in each row together. Press the seam allowances in the same direction as the other seam allowances in the row. Sew the rows together. Press the seam allowances in one direction. Set aside the remaining strip-set segments and 3" squares for the fourth border.

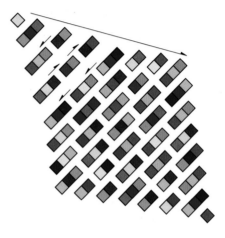

5. Straighten the edges of the pieced center block from step 4, trimming ¼" from the inside points. The block should measure 25½" x 25½".

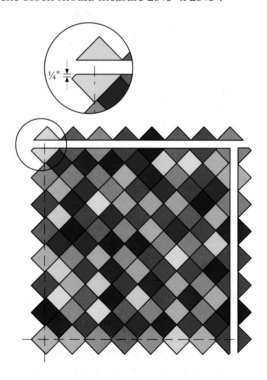

ASSEMBLING THE QUILT TOP

1. Sew the black 2" x 25½" first-border strips to the sides of the center block. Press the seam allowances toward the first border. Sew the black 2" x 28½" first-border strips to the top and bottom of the center block. Press the seam allowances toward the first border. Add the gold 10" x 28½" second-border strips to the sides of the quilt top. Press the seam allowances toward the second border. Sew the gold 10" x 47½" strips to the top and bottom of the quilt top. Press the seam allowances toward the second border. Sew the remaining black 2" x 42" third-border strips together end to end to make one long strip. From this strip, cut two strips, 2" x 47½", and two strips, 2" x 50½". Sew the 2" x 47½" strips to the sides of the quilt top, backstitching at the beginning and end of the seams to keep them from coming apart while you appliqué. Press the seam allowances toward the third border. Sew the 2" x 50½" strips to the top and bottom of the quilt top, backstitching at the beginning and end of the seams. Press the seam allowances toward the third border.

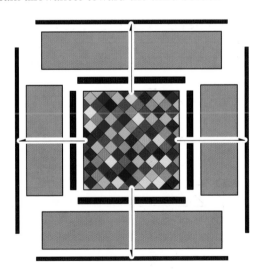

2. Refer to "Bias Vines" on page 14 for detailed instructions to prepare approximately 144" of bias vine from the green fabric. Leave enough uncut fabric to make the leaves.

3. Refer to "Fusible-Web Appliqué" on page 12 and use the patterns on page 79 to prepare the appliqués from the fabrics indicated.

4. Using the appliqué placement diagram below and the photo on page 72 as guides, pin the bias stems in place on the gold second border. Arrange the appliqué shapes and press in place. You will have four flower A shapes left over; arrange these pieces on the gold 7½" squares and press in place. Use matching thread to blanket-stitch around each shape by hand or machine. Set aside the appliquéd squares for the fourth border.

Appliqué placement

5. To make the pieced fourth-border strips, using the remaining strip-set segments from "Piecing the Center Square," arrange 17 three-square segments, 15 two-square segments, and two 3" squares into diagonal rows as shown, rotating the segments as needed so the seam allowances alternate directions from row to row. Sew the units in each row together. Press the seam allowances in the same direction as the other seam allowances in the row. Sew the rows together. Press the seam allowances in one direction. Repeat to make a total of four pieced border strips. Trim each strip in the same manner as the center block. Each border strip should measure 7½" x 50½".

Make 4.

6. Sew pieced fourth-border strips to the sides of the quilt top. Press the seam allowances toward the third border. Sew the gold 7½" appliquéd squares to the ends of the remaining two pieced border strips. Press the seam allowances toward the squares. Add these pieced border strips to the top and bottom of the quilt top. Press the seam allowances toward the third border.

7. Sew the black 3½" x 42" fifth-border strips together end to end to make one long strip. From this strip, cut two strips, 3½" x 64½", and two strips, 3½" x 70½". Sew the 3½" x 64½" strips to the sides of the quilt top. Press the seam allowances toward the fifth border. Sew the 3½" x 70½" strips to the top and bottom of the quilt top. Press the seam allowances toward the fifth border.

Quilt assembly

FINISHING THE QUILT

Refer to "Finishing Basics" on page 16 for detailed instructions as needed.

1. Layer the backing, batting, and quilt top; baste.
2. Quilt as desired. Our quilt is machine quilted with an allover design.
3. Bind the quilt using the black 2½"-wide strips.

CRANBERRY APPLE CRISP

10 cups cooking apples, cored and sliced
½ cup white sugar
1 cup plus 2 tablespoons all-purpose flour, divided
1 teaspoon ground cinnamon
1 can (14 ounces) whole-berry cranberry sauce
1 cup quick-cooking oats
1 cup packed brown sugar
½ cup butter, melted

Preheat oven to 350°. Place the sliced apples in a greased 9" x 13" pan. Mix the white sugar, 2 tablespoons flour, ground cinnamon, and cranberry sauce together. Pour over apples and mix together. Combine the oats, 1 cup flour, brown sugar, and melted butter together. Crumble evenly over the apple mixture. Bake for about 45 minutes.

Cranberry Cottage

Designed and made by Jeanne Large and Shelley Wicks; quilted by Wendy Findlay

CRANBERRY COTTAGE TABLE RUNNER

FINISHED RUNNER: 21½" x 54½"

MATERIALS

Yardage is based on 42"-wide fabrics.

⅞ yard of gold fabric for outer border and binding

5 fat eighths (9" x 21") of assorted medium-beige fabrics for background

¼ yard of dark-gold fabric for inner border

1 fat quarter (18" x 21") of green fabric for vines

6½" x 7" rectangle *each* of 5 assorted red fabrics for flower A appliqués

4½" x 18" rectangle of green fabric for flower A large-center appliqués

3½" x 12½" rectangle of brown fabric for flower A small-center appliqués

9" x 10" rectangle of green fabric #1 for leaf appliqués

6½" x 10½" rectangle of purple fabric for flower B appliqués

4½" x 7" rectangle of gold fabric for flower B center appliqués

5" x 7" rectangle of green fabric #2 for flower B base appliqués

1⅞ yards of fabric for backing

29" x 62" piece of batting

1 yard of 18"-wide lightweight paper-backed fusible web

Matching thread for appliqué

CUTTING

Cut all strips across the width of the fabric unless otherwise specified.

From *each* of the 5 assorted medium-beige fat eighths, cut:

2 strips, 3½" x 21" (10 total); crosscut into:
    1 rectangle, 3½" x 12½" (10 total)
    2 squares, 3½" x 3½" (20 total)

From the dark-gold fabric, cut:

4 strips, 2" x 42"; crosscut *1 of the strips* into 2 strips, 2" x 15½"

From the gold fabric, cut:

4 strips, 3½" x 42"
4 strips, 2½" x 42"

PIECING THE TABLE RUNNER CENTER

1. Randomly sew four of the assorted medium-beige 3½" squares together side by side. Press the seam allowances in one direction. Repeat to make a total of five pieced units that measure 3½" x 12½".

Make 5.

2. Arrange the pieced units from step 1 and the assorted medium-beige 3½" x 12½" rectangles as shown. Sew the strips together along the long edges. Press the seam allowances in one direction.

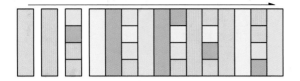

ASSEMBLING THE TABLE RUNNER TOP

1. Refer to "Bias Vines" on page 14 for detailed instruction to prepare approximately 90" of bias vine from the green fat quarter.
2. Refer to "Fusible-Web Appliqué" on page 12 and use the patterns on page 79 to prepare the appliqués from the fabrics indicated.
3. Using the appliqué placement diagram below and the photo on page 77 as guides, pin the bias vines in place on the pieced center. Arrange the appliqué shapes and press in place. Use matching thread to blanket-stitch around each shape by hand or machine.

Appliqué placement

4. Sew the remaining dark-gold 2" x 42" inner-border strips together end to end to make one long strip. From this strip, cut two strips, 2" x 45½". Sew these strips to the sides of the table runner. Press the seam allowances toward the inner border. Sew the 2" x 15½" inner-border strips to the top and bottom of the table runner. Press the seam allowances toward the inner border.
5. Sew the gold 3½" x 42" outer-border strips together end to end to make one long strip. From this strip, cut two strips, 3½" x 48½", and two strips, 3½" x 21½". Sew the 3½" x 48½"

strips to the sides of the table runner. Press the seam allowances toward the outer border. Sew the 3½" x 21½" strips to the top and bottom of the table runner. Press the seam allowances toward the outer border.

Table-runner assembly

FINISHING THE TABLE RUNNER

Refer to "Finishing Basics" on page 16 for detailed instructions as needed.

1. Layer the backing, batting, and quilt top; baste.
2. Quilt as desired. Our quilt is machine quilted with an allover design.
3. Bind the quilt using the gold 2½"-wide strips.

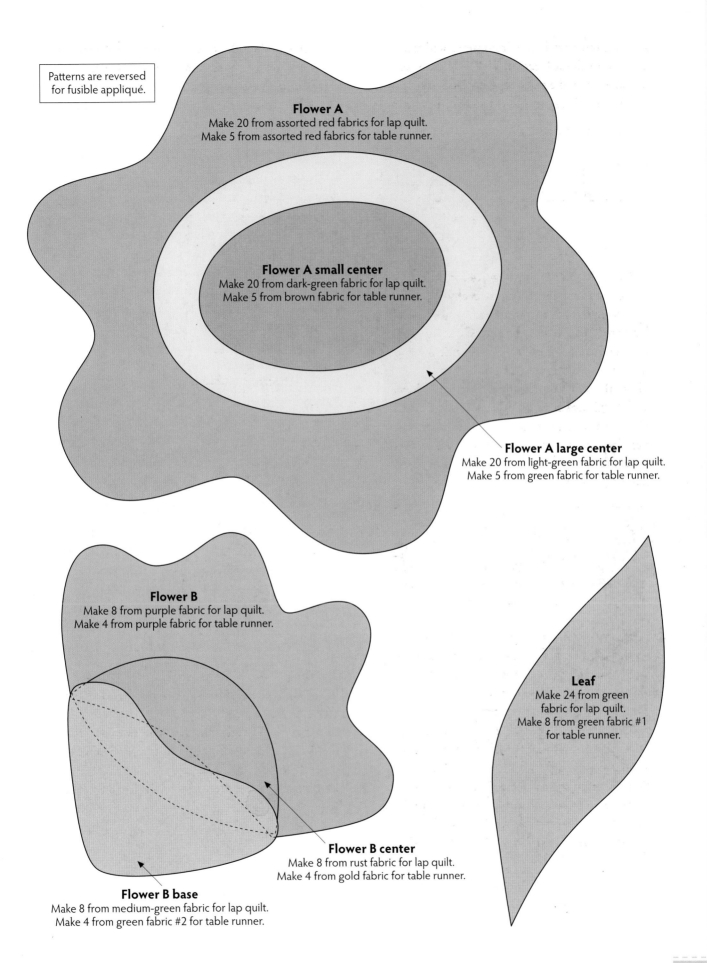

Flower A
Make 20 from assorted red fabrics for lap quilt.
Make 5 from assorted red fabrics for table runner.

Flower A small center
Make 20 from dark-green fabric for lap quilt.
Make 5 from brown fabric for table runner.

Flower A large center
Make 20 from light-green fabric for lap quilt.
Make 5 from green fabric for table runner.

Flower B
Make 8 from purple fabric for lap quilt.
Make 4 from purple fabric for table runner.

Flower B center
Make 8 from rust fabric for lap quilt.
Make 4 from gold fabric for table runner.

Flower B base
Make 8 from medium-green fabric for lap quilt.
Make 4 from green fabric #2 for table runner.

Leaf
Make 24 from green
fabric for lap quilt.
Make 8 from green fabric #1
for table runner.

Shelley Wicks and Jeanne Large have owned The Quilt Patch in Moose Jaw, Saskatchewan, Canada, for the past 10 years. In addition to the day to day running of the quilt shop, these women also design and make almost every quilt that hangs in their shop. Twice a year, spring and fall, Shelley and Jeanne unveil a brand new collection of projects with that "Urban Country" look that appeals to customers of all ages. Their customers enjoy the continuing change of quilts in the shop and know that there will always be something new to see.

With their first two books, *'Tis the Season* and *Urban Country Quilts* (Martingale, 2010 and 2011, respectively), Shelley and Jeanne introduced the chunky appliqué, easy piecing, and earth-toned projects that are the basis of their style. Their quilts give customers the confidence that each project will be something that they can accomplish easily and will look fabulous in their home.

Along with designing new projects and writing books, Shelley and Jeanne also design fabric for Clothworks Textiles. Each new step in their adventure is met head-on with passion and energy that fuels the day to day workload and fills it with laughter and fun. Both these women love life and what they do, and it shows in everything they accomplish. Find out more about Shelley and Jeanne by visiting their website: www.thequiltpatch.ca.